Alternative Approaches in Multilateral Decision Making:

Disarmament as Humanitarian Action

John Borrie and Vanessa Martin Randin
Editors

UNIDIR
United Nations Institute for Disarmament Research
Geneva, Switzerland

UNITED NATIONS

NOTE

The designations employed and the presentation of the material in this publication do not imply the expression of any opinion whatsoever on the part of the Secretariat of the United Nations concerning the legal status of any country, territory, city or area, or of its authorities, or concerning the delimitation of its frontiers or boundaries.

*

* *

The views expressed in this publication are the sole responsibility of the individual authors. They do not necessarily reflect the views or opinions of the United Nations, UNIDIR, its staff members or sponsors.

UNIDIR/2005/11

UNITED NATIONS PUBLICATION
Sales No. GV.E.05.0.8
ISBN 92-9045-172-6

The United Nations Institute for Disarmament Research (UNIDIR)—an intergovernmental organization within the United Nations—conducts research on disarmament and security. UNIDIR is based in Geneva, Switzerland, the centre for bilateral and multilateral disarmament and non-proliferation negotiations, and home of the Conference on Disarmament. The Institute explores current issues pertaining to the variety of existing and future armaments, as well as global diplomacy and local entrenched tensions and conflicts. Working with researchers, diplomats, Government officials, NGOs and other institutions since 1980, UNIDIR acts as a bridge between the research community and Governments. UNIDIR's activities are funded by contributions from Governments and donors foundations. The Institute's web site can be found at URL:

http://www.unidir.org

CONTENTS

FOREWORD

Humanitarian action is primarily taking place in areas and countries torn by war and conflict. The success of humanitarian efforts is closely linked to the success of disarmament efforts. Disarmament, or the lack it, can have dire humanitarian consequences. Disarmament and arms control processes are an integral part of promoting human security.

The 1997 Mine Ban Convention is the most recent example of a successful response to a humanitarian crisis. The process leading up to this Convention consisted of an unprecedented partnership and co-operation between governments and non-governmental and international organisations and between countries across traditional divides. These partnerships have been key to the success of the Convention, and constituted a departure from the conventional patterns that characterise protracted multilateral processes.

The purpose of UNIDIR's project *Disarmament as Humanitarian Action* is to view multilateral disarmament issues from a humanitarian angle. Disarmament and arms control problems are, at root, human security issues. This project should facilitate proposals for multilateral arms control processes that will make a real difference in terms of preventing conflict and improving people's lives.

I am encouraged by this initiative and hope that those processes that have successfully built on a broader range of voices will serve as an inspiration for everyone involved in humanitarian action.

Vidar Helgesen
State Secretary
Ministry for Foreign Affairs
Norway

ACRONYYMS

ABM	Anti-Ballistic Missile Treaty
BTWC	Bacteriological (Biological) and Toxin Weapons Convention
CAN	Climate Action Network
CCW	Convention on Certain Conventional Weapons
CD	Conference on Disarmament
CFE	Conventional Armed Forces in Europe
COP	Conference of the Parties
CTBT	Comprehensive Test Ban Treaty
CWC	Chemical Weapons Convention
ECOSOC	(United Nations) Economic and Social Council
ERW	Explosive Remnants of War
FCCC	Framework Convention on Climate Change
FCTC	Framework Convention on Tobacco Control
GHG	Green House Gas
ICBL	International Campaign to Ban Landmines
ICRC	International Committee of the Red Cross
IGO	Inter-Governmental Organization
IHL	International Humanitarian Law
ILO	International Labour Organization
INB	Intergovernmental Negotiating Body in the context of the WHO
FCTC	Framework Convention on Tobacco Control
INC	Intergovernmental Negotiating Committee
FCCC	Framework Convention on Climate Change
IPCC	Intergovernmental Panel on Climate Change
MBFR	Mutual and Balanced Force Reductions
MESCA	Group of (Me)diterranean and (Sca)ndanavian countries
NATO	North Atlantic Treaty Organisation
NGO	Non-Governmental Organization
NPT	Nuclear Non-Proliferation Treaty
PSI	Proliferation Security Initiative
UNDP	United Nations Development Programme
UNGA	United Nations General Assembly
UNIDIR	United Nations Institute for Disarmament Research
UNSC	United Nations Security Council
WHO	World Health Organization

INTRODUCTION

Multilateral disarmament and arms control negotiations are a family of processes that have achieved scant success in recent years, despite pressing political imperatives.

Examples include thwarted efforts to strengthen the Bacteriological (Biological) and Toxin Weapons Convention through legally binding measures to increase confidence in compliance, and the inability of the Conference on Disarmament to agree on a programme of work so as to begin negotiations on fissile materials (the next agreed multilateral step in the process of nuclear disarmament). The Conference, in particular, has been deadlocked since 1997 because its rules of procedure and working methods do not enable differences over priorities for negotiations to be resolved in the context of its work programme. Nor, as of writing, have efforts to move the Convention on Certain Conventional Weapons (CCW) to negotiate measures to alleviate the humanitarian effects of anti-vehicle mines (euphemistically described in that setting as mines other than anti-personnel mines) or to regulate weapons systems such as cluster munitions borne fruit.

At the same time, there have been some successes. These include the 1997 Antipersonnel Mine Ban Convention prohibiting anti-personnel mines and agreement at the end of 2003 on a protocol on explosive remnants of war in the CCW context.

Key to both successes have been humanitarian perspectives—from international organizations, field-based practitioners and transnational civil society—brought to bear on the negotiation dynamics in these processes. In particular, the implementation of the Mine Ban Convention has proved itself amenable to new—though less than revolutionary—methods of working that make porous the previously rigid partitions between "hard" security issues and humanitarianism.

Both the Mine Ban Convention and the CCW protocol negotiations on explosive remnants of war were, in practice, unique processes unlikely to be duplicated. But they are clear indications that more innovative

1

approaches in the practice of multilateral disarmament and arms control negotiation in general would be timely. In other words, a fresh look is needed if disarmament and arms control are to be effective, or considered relevant, to real world problems of this century deriving from the possession, use or threat of use of weapons. These problems range from the proliferation of small arms to potentially dangerous new "dual-use" technologies in the fields of the life sciences and nanotechnology, to spiralling proliferation of nuclear weapons. It is clearly not an easy challenge.

Against this backdrop the United Nations Institute for Disarmament Research (UNIDIR) and the United Nations Department for Disarmament Affairs (DDA) hosted a meeting to mark UNIDIR's first 20 years of existence in October 2000 entitled "Disarmament as Humanitarian Action". The meeting's theme reflected the view asserted by various actors within the disarmament/arms control spheres on the need for "human security" to be a greater driving force in multilateral efforts to disarm.

A follow-up conference co-organized with DDA and the Geneva Centre for Humanitarian Dialogue in 2002 was entitled "Disarmament, Health and Humanitarian Action: Putting People First". It highlighted the need to consider disarmament from a human security perspective because of the potentially devastating effects of the misuse of weapons on people, and because a people-first approach offers creative and practical ways to move the disarmament agenda forward.

In 2000 I wrote that the hope of UNIDIR, by helping to bring focus to human-centred approaches before the disarmament community:

> ... is to rekindle the passion required to bring about a safer and more secure world for humanity. We think that part of that process would be helped by reminding technical disarmament experts of the dire need for arms limitation and disarmament and by bringing the issue of disarmament back into the world of humanitarian action where it belongs.

However, these types of appeals or reminders are clearly insufficient on their own to regain multilateral momentum to disarm. Moreover, there is no escaping the realities that lie at the heart of contemporary difficulties in various arms control contexts. But it is also apparent that multilateral diplomats would like to avail themselves of better tools than they deploy currently to tackle the increasingly complex and (in some cases) seemingly intractable challenges they face.

In response, UNIDIR recently initiated a project with generous assistance from the Government of Norway aimed at reframing multilateral disarmament in humanitarian terms. This project is entitled "Disarmament as Humanitarian Action: Making Multilateral Negotiations Work". Based on the recognition that a greater human security focus is relevant to disarmament and arms control processes, the project is concerned with developing practical proposals on how this broad concept can be applied in functional terms to help negotiators.

This volume stems from a meeting held on 3 November 2004. The meeting introduced the Disarmament as Humanitarian Action project to a range of experts from the disarmament and humanitarian environment. That meeting outlined basic concepts behind the project. And it generated examples of alternative perspective and possible approach in order to prompt suggestions and feedback. This is especially important because the project tries to adopt practitioners' perspectives in understanding these issues.

The meeting followed Chatham House rules in order to encourage frank and open discussion. However, this volume contains papers by each of the four speakers based on their presentations, as well as a condensed summary of the meeting's subsequent discussions.

I offer a few words now about each of the volume's contributors. John Borrie, leader of the Disarmament as Humanitarian Action project, recently returned to UNIDIR after a year-and-a-half stint with the Mines-Arms Unit of the International Committee of the Red Cross (ICRC). Prior to that he was a Research Fellow at UNIDIR between September 2002 and April 2003. During that period he researched and wrote *A Global Survey of Explosive Remnants of War*, which was published by Landmine Action (UK), and which was fed into the CCW negotiations on a protocol on explosive remnants of war in June 2003. Previously John was Deputy Head of Mission for Disarmament in Geneva with the New Zealand government, and was involved with most facets of disarmament and arms control in his role there. In this volume he has written about Rethinking Multilateral Negotiations: Disarmament as Humanitarian Action.

Dr Robin Coupland is adviser on armed violence and the effects of weapons for ICRC. He became a Fellow of the Royal College of Surgeons and joined the ICRC in 1987, working as a field surgeon in many countries, and holds a graduate diploma in international law from the University of Melbourne in Australia. Robin has published medical textbooks about care for wounded people and many articles relating to the surgical management of war wounds, the effects of weapons and armed violence.

As part of his current position Robin has focused on the effects of conventional and anti-personnel weapons and has developed a health-oriented approach to a variety of issues relating to the design and use of weapons. He has paid particular attention to the effects of anti-personnel mines and fragment injuries and the disruption of bullets using the Red Cross wound classification.

In promoting the concept of armed violence as a health issue, Robin's work pertains to a number of international legal issues and in particular the responsibility of governments to review new weapons and weapons' systems. He has developed an analytical framework of armed violence as a tool for reporting and communication. He has drawn on these themes in his article on modelling armed violence: a tool for humanitarian dialogue in disarmament and arms control.

Dr Patrick McCarthy is Coordinator of the Geneva Forum, a joint initiative of the Quaker United Nations Office in Geneva, UNIDIR and the Programme for Strategic and International Security Studies of the Graduate Institute of International Studies. Geneva Forum seeks to advance disarmament and arms control processes in a number of areas. Before joining the Geneva Forum in 2000 he worked for the Organization for Security and Co-operation in Europe (OSCE) in Kosovo in the areas of human rights, democratization and election preparation and was the Conflict Prevention Coordinator of the 1999 "Hague Appeal for Peace". Patrick has a PhD in political and social sciences from the European University Institute in Florence, Italy. He has taken advantage of his unique vantage point at the intersection of arms control and humanitarian issues to write about deconstructing disarmament: the challenge of making the disarmament machinery responsive to the humanitarian imperative.

Vanessa Martin Randin is a researcher on the Disarmament as Humanitarian Action team. Prior to joining UNIDIR in 2003 Vanessa was a

Rotary Fellow at Lancaster University in the United Kingdom, where she completed her MA in international relations and strategic studies. She also holds a degree from the University of Western Ontario in Canada. Together with John Borrie, she presents findings from a research study as part of the Disarmament as Humanitarian Action Project entitled "A comparison between arms control and other multilateral negotiation processes".

On behalf of the authors and myself I would like to thank the following people and institutions for their advice or assistance in the process of preparing this volume and the meeting that inspired it: the Ministry of Foreign Affairs of Norway (particularly Ambassador Steffen Kongstad, May-Elin Stener, Gro Nystuen and Merete Lundemo), Daniel Prins of the Permanent Mission of the Netherlands to the Conference on Disarmament in Geneva, Christophe Carle, Nicolas Gérard, Kerstin Vignard, Derek Miller, Isabelle Roger, Anita Blétry, Talayeh Voosoghi, Gustavo Laurie and John Flanagan of the United Nations Mine Action Service, the staff of DDA—both in New York and in Geneva—David Atwood of the Quaker United Nations Office in Geneva, Ambassador Tim Caughley and Hinewai Loose of the Permanent Mission of New Zealand in Geneva, the Mines-Arms Unit team in the Legal Division of ICRC, Bo Kjellén, Juhanni Lönnroth, the World Health Organization Framework Convention Team on the Tobacco-Free Initiative (particularly Douglas Bettcher, Gemma Vestal and Marta Seoane) and Brook Boyer of the United Nations Institute for Training and Research.

Patricia Lewis
Director
UNIDIR

CHAPTER 1

RETHINKING MULTILATERAL NEGOTIATIONS: DISARMAMENT AS HUMANITARIAN ACTION

John Borrie

Increasing attention has been focused in recent years on the need for multilateral negotiation processes in the disarmament and arms control field to "think outside the box" in addressing contemporary challenges. But beyond recognition that there are imperfections in current approaches, it is not always clear that the parameters of the existing box are sufficiently understood or, indeed, what these new approaches should be in practical terms. This introductory paper considers some of the assumptions that negotiating practitioners in the multilateral disarmament and arms control field currently hold—among them orthodox notions of national security and "political will"—and questions whether they are always sufficient or appropriate in framing effective multilateral responses.[1] Several different ideas are unpacked (ideas that might initially appear disparate) pointing to some avenues for follow-up in order to assist negotiating practitioners in their work.

Security thinking in the context of multilateral arms control and disarmament has, at least until lately, been dominated by security concepts focusing on external threats to states and, in particular, threats posed by other states. While traditional forms of inter-state military conflict appear (at least for now) to be on the wane, a host of other scenarios involving insecurity and violent conflict are burgeoning in the twenty-first century. These range from transnational violent threats associated with terrorism, trafficking in people and illicit goods, ethnic and communal conflict to the total failure and breakdown of certain states' internal order.

Beyond their immediate and local effects, the consequences of these forms of conflict can be amplified widely because of the increasing inter-connectedness of the international system, as recognized in the recent report of the United Nations Secretary-General's High-Level Panel on Threats, Challenges and Change.[2] The international system is, for its part, encountering real difficulties in dealing effectively with collective security problems through the usual multilateral arms control and disarmament mechanisms. This lack of progress ultimately has serious human consequences.

At the same time, alternative perspectives have evolved in order to contextualize and devise solutions to problems associated with violent conflict. The United Nations Development Programme (UNDP) *Human Development Report 1994* is generally regarded as a watershed in this regard, incorporating as it did a broad view of "human security" focusing on the security of the individual, rather than of the traditional unit of security—that of the state.[3] A myriad of human security definitions have emerged since then, to the extent that more than a decade later there is no general agreement about what the term means in functional terms, let alone how it should be applied.

Nevertheless, human security and humanitarian approaches to problem-solving do have utility in assisting practitioners in multilateral arms control and disarmament negotiations. This has been shown, for instance, by their limited application in the Antipersonnel Mine Ban Convention process, the 2003 protocol on explosive remnants of war and in the context of combating illicit trade in small arms and light weapons.[4] These approaches differ from the ways in which practitioners in multilateral arms control and disarmament traditionally view issues of security. In orthodox disarmament and arms control negotiating environments the state—not the individual—is the sole referent point for achieving and reaping security benefits.

This "national security" referent point remains relevant and important. Nor is it likely to be eclipsed while the nation state remains the basic unit of international order. But new and complex challenges of security this century, such as small arms and light weapons proliferation and reducing the risk of advances in the life sciences being turned to hostile use, increasingly call for supplementary perspectives in order for them to be addressed effectively. Humanitarian perspectives and concepts can constitute certain of these supplements. They do not need to be viewed as exclusive alternatives to national security approaches in order to assist negotiating practitioners and can help build common ground in responding to collective challenges in security, especially as states are responsible for contributing to their citizens' security in individual and communal terms, as well as from external threats posed by other states.

To help assist negotiators, UNIDIR recently initiated a project aimed at reframing multilateral disarmament and arms control issues in humanitarian terms from a problem-solving perspective. The project will analyse practitioners' viewpoints in arms control and disarmament processes and suggest new concepts, tools and techniques that might assist them. Hence the project's title—Disarmament as Humanitarian Action: Making Multilateral Negotiations Work.

Answering questions about what makes some negotiations in arms control and disarmament more successful than others (and, indeed, what even constitutes success) is not easy. Nor is it the purpose of this introductory paper. Instead, some basic parameters are introduced here and we outline what we mean by "reframing" multilateral disarmament and arms control as humanitarian action.

TERMS OF REFERENCE

As the first step to doing so, it is important to explain what is meant by terms such as disarmament, arms control and humanitarian action, as used here. Disarmament, for example, is a term that carries various connotations. For our purposes it is "the traditional term for the elimination, as well as the limitation or reduction (through negotiation of an international agreement) of the means by which nations wage war".[5]

It should be noted that disarmament and arms control are not supposed to be interchangeable terms, although they are sometimes used as such. Arms control was a term originally coined in the 1950s referring to international agreements intended to limit the arms race between the United States and the Soviet Union. It was recognized that these activities—limiting, rather than reversing arms competition—differed from disarmament because general and complete disarmament did not seem readily achievable at the time. Non-proliferation is also a term that has been in use since at least the 1960s, and falls within the umbrella concept of arms control.[6]

Defining humanitarian action or assistance is trickier. In fact, these overlapping concepts possess no generally agreed definitions. A recent international meeting of humanitarian negotiators concluded that this was not necessarily a problem from a practical perspective, however. "There had always been different forms of humanitarianism and it had not been proven whether the lack of identity has had a bad impact on humanitarian work."[7] For our purposes humanitarian action can be defined as an inclusive term connoting activities that stem from rules or principles of international humanitarian law (IHL), also known as "the laws of war".[8]

An intrinsic link exists between disarmament, arms control and international humanitarian law:

> All laws of war suffer from one common weakness: the rules of conduct established for belligerents in time of peace may not resist the pressure of military expedience generated in the course of hostilities, and the attempts to "humanise war" may sometimes prove futile. The danger that the weapons prohibited may, under certain circumstances be resorted to—as has occurred on several occasions—will not disappear as long as these weapons remain in the arsenals of States. Hence the intrinsic link between the development of the humanitarian laws of war and progress in the field of disarmament.[9]

On this basis "one could argue that if the principle of distinction or the prohibition on the use of weapons which cause superfluous injury or unnecessary suffering had been respected by all belligerents, disarmament and arms control treaties would be less necessary".[10]

A defining feature of the modern era of armed conflict is humanity's capacity to extinguish itself as a species. Merely the existence of nuclear or biological weapons, for instance, is destabilizing and their use could have terrible consequences. The ever-real potential for escalation of conventional armed conflict to use of so-called weapons of mass destruction necessitates acknowledging that continuum of armed violence, and the requirement for ways to alleviate or prevent such escalation. Disarmament and arms control and IHL have important roles to play in this context.[11]

MULTILATERALISM AND ITS DISCONTENTS

Despite the pressing need for the enforcement, consolidation and further strengthening of such norms, however, some important multilateral disarmament and arms control processes—like the Conference on Disarmament—have lately become moribund. Others like the Ad Hoc Group of states parties to the Bacteriological (Biological) and Toxin Weapons Convention (BTWC) (tasked with negotiating a verification protocol to that treaty), have been rejected or superseded by less robust processes. This has led to questioning by some of the value of multilateral disarmament and arms control.

Moreover, the period since the terror attacks of 11 September 2001 has seen a recasting of many security responses at the state level as elements of an international "war on terror". There are sound reasons for this new emphasis. But, still, the change in emphasis can obscure the reality that states, and the international community at large, remain vulnerable to threats to their security from other states, not only from armed non-state actors like Al-Qaeda.

The change of emphasis has benefited some multilateral forums, though. The United Nations Security Council, for example, has enhanced its institutional role in coordinating non-proliferation against weapons of mass destruction by means of its resolution 1540. This resolution established a Committee of the Security Council for at least two years in order to monitor the resolution's implementation "and to this end calls upon States to present a first report no later than six months from the adoption of this resolution to the Committee on steps they have taken or intend to take to implement this resolution".[12] New types of collective response have also emerged such as the United States-led Proliferation Security Initiative (PSI), which stresses "practical cooperation" by PSI partners in physical interdiction efforts against weapons of mass destruction.[13] The importance of other innovations, such as Cooperative Threat Reduction measures to reduce proliferation risks in the countries of the former Soviet Union, have been reaffirmed.

However, it is significant that these new frameworks for potential action are founded upon existing norms including the Nuclear Non-Proliferation Treaty (NPT), BTWC and the Chemical Weapons Convention (CWC). This relationship is alluded to in Security Council resolution 1540—

although the resolution's text skirts the issue of how comfortably its enhanced role sits with existing review processes under these treaties that include all of their respective memberships and which are more representative than the limited membership of the Security Council. With respect to the role of the PSI its chief advocate, the United States, contends that "the foundation of our ability to act in support of PSI activities is our respective national legal authorities and relevant international frameworks".[14] This is combined with an insistence by Washington that PSI is an activity *not a process* in the face of "a much larger set of apprehensions and uncertainties that have rightfully stirred doubts that the PSI will indeed contribute to non-proliferation goals without undermining international peace and cooperation".[15]

What has *not* changed is that further normative enhancement of international norms—as opposed to just their enforcement—will require multilateral structures for legitimacy, if not for substantive development. Even if collective disarmament and arms control processes have been partially eclipsed by other types of response, they remain commonly agreed benchmarks among a wide spectrum of the international community. Other types of response that lie between the national and broadly multilateral in the international security domain are not necessarily incompatible. But the maintenance and further development of multilateral disarmament and arms control norms are probably indispensable if these other levels of response are to be effective.

Ultimately, disarmament and arms control negotiation developed because of the need for states to enhance their security collectively, primarily for protection from one another. Despite terrorism representing a dominant theme at present, the need to develop multilateral agreements among states on common norms will remain.[16]

Strong calls have been heard from entities such as the High-Level Panel on Threats, Challenges and Change for strengthening the most visible multilateral structure—the United Nations system—through institution-building. And the Panel calls for greater support by member states to reinvigorate multilateral problem-solving in international security.[17] This is important, but not the whole solution. Answers need to be found to underlying questions of *how* momentum to succeed can be brought back to multilateral disarmament and arms control by helping existing processes to start moving again. Otherwise new processes needlessly risk becoming mired in similar difficulties to current ones.

These issues are especially pertinent in the wake of the re-election in the United States of George W. Bush for a second presidential term. Responding to accusations that it is increasingly unilateralist (or is at least turning away from multilateral forms of international security response) the United States has insisted that it *is* still committed to multilateralism—but will not support negotiating outcomes it does not perceive to be within its definition of the United States' national interest.[18] Both these contrasting perceptions point to the need to ensure that multilateral disarmament and arms control responses are tuned to function more effectively in order to make them more attractive as venues for substantive engagement to solve international security-related problems.

Common sense suggests that, just as sustainable enhancements to international security need the legitimacy that collective multilateral norms can bestow, it is unrealistic to expect key players in the international system, like the United States, to remain committed to multilateral processes when they perceive their vital interests threatened because these lack responsiveness or adaptability. In the longer term, failure to address such criticisms will merely add validity to them, which benefits nobody. "A conscious strategy of multilateral engagement implies a commitment to correcting these deficiencies and improving the emerging framework of global cooperation. It means designing strategies that maximise the benefits of working with others while minimizing the costs and constraints."[19]

POLITICAL WILL

Making multilateralism more effective is certainly easier said than done. Examining factors associated with multilateral negotiations and the ways in which they interact is one place to start in considering how to making it so. Some specific observations to this end are presented later in this volume.[20] A better understanding of how negotiations work—or fail to work—in practice may also cast light on the various phenomena often described as comprising "political will", which is a term often used by multilateral diplomats. But it is questionable whether political will is a concept useful in analysing their dynamics because referring to political will is like describing the weather on a particular day as the product of the forces of nature: it rather states the obvious and conveys little in the way of useful insight or description.

For all of its deficiencies, however, political will remains firmly part of the lexicon of the disarmament and arms control negotiator. As a shorthand term this is fine. In recent years, however, "lack of political will" has become elevated to the status of an explanation in itself for lack of progress in disarmament and arms control when it is merely a sign pointing to specific obstacles or postures that make effective negotiating outcomes more difficult to achieve.

As indicated above, the reality is that while orthodox multilateral processes have suffered in recent years some other collective responses, like the PSI, have nevertheless been undertaken and may prove quite successful. Even among those states least inclined to use the orthodox multilateral disarmament and arms control machinery, therefore, *there are still extraordinary efforts at the bilateral and plurilateral levels*. This indicates that we are not confronted by a situation of apathy. Rather, political attention and energy are being diverted into channels other than traditional multilateral disarmament and arms control forums.

Although they are more formal terms than political will, disarmament, arms control and humanitarian assistance are, nevertheless, also concepts that have to reflect political imperatives and be elastic enough to be fitted around various contexts for the policymakers and negotiators using them. Consequently they are difficult to test by means of falsification: there are no hard-and-fast rules about what may or may not qualify for consideration within the disarmament, arms control and humanitarian spheres, apart from political acceptability. In a post-11 September world this has already proved more malleable than it was perceived to be previously.

Unlike political will, however, these terms function as descriptions in the context of multilateral dynamics, not as explanations for them. Correspondingly they remain relevant provided they help negotiators conceptualize problems and possible ways to solutions. They lose their value as useful concepts if their boundaries or other characteristics become too confining.

Disarmament, arms control and humanitarian assistance have further value. They help to create (or, in the best cases, to preserve) links between negotiating practitioners in the disarmament and arms control field with wider constituencies, for example in transnational civil society, in order to enable the latter to understand and mobilize on issues of concern to them in ways relevant to influencing the direction of negotiating processes.

By contrast, explanations of negotiating processes or dynamics predicated simply on perceived levels of political will tend, in practice, to obscure rather than aid transparency to those outside them. This is not helpful in ensuring accountability of policymakers and negotiators to their domestic constituencies or to broader international public opinion. Nor does it help negotiating practitioners distinguish features of their working environment that are intentionally caused by features that were not intended or "designed" into the operation of the system, but arose for other reasons.

A COMMUNITY OF PRACTICE

Rather than couching analysis in terms of political will then, it may be more useful to consider disarmament and arms control negotiators interacting in multilateral forums as members of a distinctive "community of practice".

What does this mean? For our purposes a community of practice simply entails "a group of people who over a period of time share in some set of social practices geared toward some common social purpose".[21] Some of these practices, such as titles, formal rules of negotiating procedure and other working methods—are formal. Some other practices—perennial coffee breaks, "off-the-record" working lunches and dinners as well as the art of fobbing off dull colleagues at diplomatic receptions, for instance—are informal. But an understanding of what they are, how they work and the roles and responsibilities of members is implicitly shared in that community. It is what connects a group of individuals. But it is also what sets them apart from others. This community of practice, however loose and amorphous it may be perceived to be, is what fashions negotiating outcomes within various parameters.

The concept of a community of practice outlined above is also useful because it is a way of viewing multilateral negotiators as more than simply mouthpieces of their governments. It recognizes that their interactions are dynamic. The exploitation of these dynamics makes negotiation and compromise possible at the multilateral level in the pursuit of policy outcomes.

Moreover, examining these issues in terms of the functioning of a community of practice allows the possibility of structural problems arising in—and across—multilateral disarmament and arms control processes for reasons that are not premeditated in political or diplomatic terms. To put this another way: if we accept that diplomatic and multilateral practices *evolve* over time for reasons other than those designed intentionally, then it follows that some aspects of the community of practice are *not* designed. This can result in dynamics or practices that are unproductive, and which were unintended. In political-will explanations the absence of political will has logically to be the product of premeditated agency—it has to be "somebody's fault". (There is "will" or "lack of will"—"anti-will", if you like—or the "wrong kind of will", which all presuppose conscious agency.) But sometimes there is simply no identifiable culprit for problems or inefficiencies.

The idea of a community of practice should not be a great conceptual leap for diplomatic practitioners. Most already recognize the existence of differences between their informal and formal methods of interaction when they speak, for instance, about "personality", "atmospherics" or "negotiating room dynamics" as x-factors in negotiations. These labels also point to the fact that negotiation processes in the disarmament and arms control context are highly iterative. That is, they are affected by many different variables that dispose their dynamics to further change on a continuous basis.

Iterative negotiating dynamics, in themselves, are not sufficient to constitute a community of practice. That is because some of the variables of a negotiation process may be unique to it and reflect particular sensitivities of the parties or dimensions of the substance of the negotiation, which will not be duplicated again. But other variables are likely to be common to disarmament and arms control negotiators' community of practice across various processes—especially as legal and diplomatic precedent usually guide them and the same people often work in different negotiations. Examples include rules of procedure and regional group structures (in forums such as the Conference on Disarmament) and the cohesive attitudes or ideologies of states or groups of states in their negotiating interaction. They shape iterative negotiating dynamics and are recursive in different processes to the extent that they cumulatively reflect and contribute to negotiators' community of practice. This, in turn, helps to constitute diplomatic precedent.

It follows that while some negotiating variables are visible at the level of the narrative, others only become fully visible by observing negotiating interaction over longer time frames and in the context of broader comparison of various negotiating processes. This does not mean that narrative explanations for specific multilateral disarmament and arms control processes are incompatible with other forms of analysis. But such narratives are unlikely to be complete on their own because changes in the character of their community of practice may be all but imperceptible to disarmament and arms control negotiators, journalists and statespeople in one process or brief time frame. This is especially so because membership of this community tends to be highly fluid, with individual participants also being members of other cross-cutting communities of practice—civil services being one—that see them move in and out at frequent intervals.

COMPLEXITY

While the evolution of a community of practice is usually gradual in terms of the work spans of its individual members, broader changes in the international security context may be rapid and far-reaching. Indeed it has become a common cliché that we live in a globalizing world, which is another way to say it is more interconnected. The consequences of increasing interconnectedness, in conjunction with continuous technological advance, are profound for the maintenance and development of international security by multilateral means.[22]

First, instantaneous communications create new pressures on negotiators to compress information-processing and decision-making time. And there is increasing potential for scrutiny of day-to-day diplomatic negotiating activities and interaction by their governments (as well as others, by means of espionage, for instance). Modern technologies such as the ubiquitous mobile phone, hand-held wireless e-mail devices and jet air travel can be double-edged swords. They enable a negotiator to gain access to distant resources and sources of information more easily. Conversely they lose their value if these links become a straitjacket restricting object-oriented responses flexible enough to capitalize on opportunities emerging from negotiating dynamics (of "being in the room") of which authorities at home may not be fully cognizant.

Secondly, many of the issues requiring multilateral responses in the field of disarmament and arms control are increasingly complex and interdependent. Illicit small arms and light weapons proliferation, for instance, is potentially global in scope. But even a cursory look reveals a complex mosaic of different situations that defy straightforward characterization at a global level. There are no simple answers as to why individuals or groups across a broad range of different societies want to get guns or to use—or threaten to use—them to kill or injure other human beings. The presence of accumulations of automatic weapons in civilian settings in many societies is a menace to stability and safety, but the linkage is not automatic.[23] Solutions that simply address the characteristics of these weapons (which are similar in technical design the world over) without considering contextual factors such as poverty and lack of economic opportunity, for instance, are therefore likely to fail in addressing complex phenomena like illicit small arms and light weapons proliferation that affect (and reflect) the behaviour of many individuals and groups within different societies.

The international humanitarian law and disarmament and arms control domains, for their part, developed in the nineteenth and twentieth centuries as corollaries of security diplomacy at the inter-state level, rather than at the individual or community levels. The basic unit of this diplomacy, the nation state, was recognized as early as the Peace of Westphalia in 1648 at the conclusion of the devastating European Thirty Years' War, although the term "national security" as understood in the modern sense was not used until after the Second World War.[24] Nevertheless, the Westphalian Peace is generally seen as a watershed because it signalled a shift in the character of power struggles from the religious to the secular. Such a shift resulted in the development of inter-state relations along lines dictated by national "interest" or power to an increasing extent as time passed. The development and the centralization of power within European nation states itself reflected the exigencies of waging war (or of possessing the capability to make war) in a geopolitical environment in which potential adversaries were doing the same.[25]

Historians usually date the early days of recognizably multilateral diplomacy from the convening of the European "great Powers" in the

Concert of Europe in 1815 after the defeat of Napoleon. Although diplomatic negotiation in the nineteenth century involved men of different nationalities (and they were virtually always men) they came from similar classes, backgrounds, interests and outlooks. Moreover, in a world in which communication was usually limited to the pace of a horse, sailing ship or slow steam train most geopolitical issues such as wars unfolded over weeks or months.

Nor was the international system multilateral in the sense to which we are accustomed today. Until decolonization began in earnest in the middle of the twentieth century there were only a handful of great Powers. This made negotiating interaction much more manageable in its number of variables than the 190 or so countries belonging to the United Nations today. A few countries, a few people, a few languages, common histories and understandings of what constituted "diplomacy" all helped to cement a common community of perceptions and attitudes towards negotiating interaction.[26] Nor did the influence of the media, while growing, have the same impact that it does today.

Scholars identify varying phases or transitions in the development of multilateral diplomacy. Some perceive a shift from traditional diplomacy based on the principles of Europe's nineteenth-century balance of power to Wilsonian ideals of "open diplomacy". However, such transitions can be (and are) contested: Lippman, Morgenthau and Kissinger are examples of better known so-called "realists". Indeed, the realist school's conception of national security has dominated the development of security thinking both in the "strategic" policymaking community and in the multilateral sphere since the 1940s until at least the late 1980s.[27] Today theoretical frameworks abound for interpreting and analysing the direction of the international system and approaches to achieving security from "clashes of civilizations" (Huntington), "America is from Mars, Europe is from Venus" (Kagan) to an emerging "empire lite" of imperial and humanitarian intervention by the world's leading Powers (Ignatieff), to name but a few contemporary examples.[28]

One way to consider the substance of disarmament and arms control negotiations as they developed through the twentieth century would be to describe them as generally *reductionist* rather than synthetic. All this means is that as disarmament and arms control's community of practice gradually developed it tended to do so along lines that broke down complicated problems into their constituent elements. Specialists were brought in to deal with technical or military issues within negotiations. Oversight at the diplomatic and political level was supposed to keep this aligned with the broader picture. Reductionism was not so much a driver in interaction between states in terms of their security as a means to help them achieve it.

This "orthodox" model was, and continues to be, very powerful. It is especially useful in circumstances in which each negotiating actor has the time and resources to study and understand the postures of its negotiating counterparts. Moreover, the nature of a number of twentieth-century disarmament and arms control negotiations meant that they could be divided up productively in such a reductionist manner. Examples include nuclear reduction measures agreed between the United States and the Soviet Union, the Conventional Forces in Europe agreement and the CWC negotiations.[29] These agreements all contain discrete components, lists— whether of bombers, tanks, nuclear warheads or toxic chemicals—and are rationally organized to solve concrete problems of identification, verification and other aspects of arms control or disarmament.

Sometimes for practical or political reasons the reductionist tendency could only be taken so far, though. Agreements such as the 1972 BTWC looked very different, for instance, from the CWC agreed later. In the BTWC case the means of verification to ensure confidence in compliance with its prohibitions lagged behind the political commitment underpinning its negotiation. Consequently, beyond containing general undertakings and prohibitions, the BTWC is very general in its drafting—legally binding statements of intent without provision for verification or other measures intended to promote confidence in compliance.[30]

The contrast between reductionist and synthetic modes outlined above is, of course, oversimplified. But it serves to illustrate a limitation of traditional approaches to disarmament and arms control; that they can be confounded when there are too many different but interacting factors to analyse. As mentioned above, new disarmament challenges this century are increasingly characterized by the interdependence of myriad variables, rather than the innate strategic qualities of specific objects or systems. The interaction of these variables creates emergent properties in the international security system, which are not necessarily seen by taking the system apart and examining each of its constituent elements. The *non-*

linearity of some of these interactions is something that may be profoundly counter-intuitive to diplomatic negotiators.[31]

Two differing examples help to illustrate this point. First, a lot of technology with proliferation potential for biological weapons is inherently "dual-use". This means that hostile use of the life sciences is largely a question of intent rather than access to special materials or equipment. Biological weapons can potentially be made with quite basic materials and knowledge usually used for peaceful purposes. "Biotechnology is becoming cheaper, and knowledge of it more widespread. The place that the life sciences occupy in society is widening."[32] Most societies find it excessively difficult or inconvenient to prohibit or regulate access to these technologies too restrictively, especially as they usually have considerable benefits for society when used legitimately.

The life sciences will continue to advance and increasingly permeate society in ways analogous to the far-reaching changes to society that the integration of electronic microprocessors wrought in recent decades. This means the proliferation signature of biological weapons is certain to change. It follows that understanding and minimizing hostile *intent* will become as relevant to efforts in strengthening norms against biological weapons at least as much as simply regulating access to the technologies themselves.

Some of these advances in the life sciences of potential risk for misuse by those with hostile intent are concurrently becoming more *intangible* in form. Examples already exist: the genetic sequencing of a number of viruses such as polio and some members of the orthopox virus family means that they can (and have) been reconstructed synthetically in laboratories using common materials without an original sample of the pathogen being needed.[33] Synthesis of bacteria is predicted to follow.[34]

This greater intangibility of life science technologies of potential relevance to hostile use is likely to have profound implications for non-proliferation efforts in the long term, especially as auxiliary laboratory technologies also become more affordable and widespread. Moreover, scientific and technical knowledge is also diffusing in new ways (like over the Internet) that may not afford close supervision. This convergence of factors invites the likelihood that hostile use of the life sciences will come about for flippant or casual reasons involving misplaced curiosity or lack of awareness by individuals about the consequences of their actions, as the development and spread of computer viruses already occur now.[35]

A second example, that of illicit small arms and light weapons proliferation, also poses complex challenges, as discussed earlier. But the characteristics of this proliferation—its causes, progression and consequences—although complex, differ in nature from hostile use of the life sciences. Indeed, this issue is perhaps most usefully seen as a cluster of overlapping concerns based on the understanding that the presence of these weapons in post-conflict situations, or in large concentrations in any society, can be profoundly detrimental.

A characteristic of small arms and light weapon proliferation problems in distinct environments is their potential for interconnection. Weapons slosh from conflict to conflict, possession by non-state actors can become widespread, and their humanitarian consequences—forced migration, ethnic cleansing, refugee crises—may take on regional and international dimensions. "Even if one could turn off the small arms tap tomorrow, they would continue to circulate between conflicts, communities and combatants. This is because the diffusion of small arms takes place at the interface of global and local arenas, in situations of inequality and insecurity, posing intricate challenges to national, regional and international actors."[36] For example, "because of their long life span, small arms are continuously recycled from old conflicts. AK-47s and M-16s used by combatants during the Vietnam War have resurfaced as far afield as Nicaragua and El Salvador more than 30 years later. Highly durable, they frequently outlast peace-agreements and can be taken up again well after the conflict has ended".[37] These complex and interconnected characteristics that may defy uniform responses globally call for greater understanding by negotiating practitioners.

In sum, it is not difficult to see why the multilateral disarmament and arms control community, grounded in a national security paradigm, is encountering mounting problems in situations of increasing complexity and interdependence in which the state is not the only, or even the most relevant, unit of analysis or decision-making. This is partly because (as was explained above) its community of practice evolves gradually. It may also be due to limits of understanding among practitioners about the ramifications of these changes for their work. Or, more likely, it may be due to difficulties in knowing how to operationalize this awareness in negotiating terms.

HUMAN SECURITY?

It is time now to return to "human security" concepts. As noted above, there is no agreed definition of what human security is. A recent survey of 21 scholars in the humanitarian security field revealed a wide range of notions of how it is most suitably defined, from a "bridge between the interconnected challenges confronting the world", "psycho-social well-being over time" to "a concept in search of relevance".[38]

If human security lacks a consensus meaning, what use is it for analysis and decision-making? Those who believe human security approaches have utility note that human security takes the perspective of the individual and of the community, rather than the nation state. A further hallmark of human security approaches and, indeed, of humanitarian responses in general, is the degree to which they recognize interlinkages between different domains, both within and beyond the traditional elements of national security. Successful humanitarian response is inherently multidisciplinary. It is in this sense that concepts deployed or originating in the humanitarian sector may provide useful frameworks for tackling disarmament and arms control challenges: human security concepts are different wavelengths at which to view disarmament and arms control problems.

There is, however, divergence between so-called "narrow" and "broad" conceptions of human security. UNDP, for instance, established a broad concept with seven components: economic, food, health, environmental, personal, community and political security. In the same groundbreaking *Human Development Report 1994* the authors argued that "the concept of security has for too long been interpreted narrowly: as security of territory from external aggression, or as protection of national interests in foreign policy or as global security from the threat of a nuclear holocaust. It has been related more to nation-states than to people".[39] Overall, the UNDP concept "acknowledged the imperative for multi-faceted and human-centred security in daily life and the conviction that the search for stability lay in development rather than in arms".[40] While differentiating human security from human development the UNDP concept of human security was nevertheless very broad in scope.

There are valid criticisms of broad human security approaches. One is that the broader the definition the less useful it is as a basis for analysis and response by the policymaking community, which includes the community of practice of multilateral negotiators. (This is at the crux of the author's difficulty with the Commission on Human Security's conceptualization of human security in terms of a "vital core".)[41] By contrast, proponents of "narrow" concepts of human security focus on evaluating the effects of violent threats as a basis for policy response. They argue that only narrow conceptions have resulted in successful international initiatives using human security parameters. These initiatives include the Mine Ban Convention, the International Criminal Court, as well as the recent international focus on child soldiers, small arms and the role of non-state actors in conflict.[42]

A criticism of these narrower human security approaches is that they can be so pragmatic that they risk losing their analytic clarity and distinctiveness. An additional reservation is that while the results of processes such as the Mine Ban Convention negotiations and small arms might be perceived as outcomes of human security approaches (and certainly have been talked up as such by its supporters), it does not automatically follow that this actually *did* guide negotiators at the time, who often had rather more prosaic concerns. The author (a governmental participant in the subsequent Mine Ban Convention process as well as in the drafting of the 2001 programme of action on illicit trade in small arms and light weapons) remains to be convinced that human security ideas did more than inform the views of those negotiators *already openly disposed towards them* in the turmoil of drafting and deal-making. Nevertheless, it represents a real benefit that human security provided a more coherent intellectual framework for framing issues and negotiating on substance in these contexts. In the Mine Ban Convention context, for instance, it enabled a shared analysis between donor and mine-affected countries to develop and consequently generate money and resources for mine action assistance.

Lately there have been efforts in the human security field to attempt to move beyond disagreement about its broad and narrow conceptions. Some have developed further ideas, such as "thresholds-based" definitions "to let the actual risks determine what human security is not. From this, a regionally defined human security measure can be produced. This stays true to the original focus of the concept but renders it analytically and practically useful for addressing today's climate of insecurity."[43]

Regardless of the ongoing debate, field-based perspectives brought to bear by the humanitarian community in multilateral disarmament and arms control processes have been at least as important as any contribution of human security theory. Multilateral action on anti-personnel mines, small arms and light weapons and explosive remnants of war were all pre-dated, and partly stemmed from, concerns expressed by international agencies, non-governmental organizations (NGOs) and individuals working at post-conflict environments about the effects of these weapons on individuals and the communities to which they belonged. In the case of anti-personnel mines these concerns motivated actors, such as the International Committee of the Red Cross (ICRC), to begin collating data on the injuries caused by these weapons, which in turn helped to establish empirically the case for their abolition and the multilateral negotiating processes that followed.[44]

The humanitarian community's perspective—that the presence and use of anti-personnel mines causes insecurity and acts as an impediment to development—ultimately made sense to the majority of the international policymaking community and in a form that could be acted upon. Not only was it analytically useful in framing the problem of anti-personnel mines, this humanitarian orientation helped to break down splits by political grouping, particularly between North and South, that are common features of disarmament and arms control processes.[45]

The efficacy of a humanitarian framing of the anti-personnel mine problem and potential solution was also confirmed by empirical data of the effects of these mines and by dynamic contact between mine action practitioners with multilateral negotiators. As Don Hubert pointed out:

> … it was precisely [anti-personnel mines'] widespread use that provided the evidence on which to build the campaign … Campaigners directly affected by mines included mine victims, deminers and medical staff tasked with assisting victims. Collectively they had unparalleled expertise and made compelling spokespersons who could not be easily dismissed by politicians, diplomats or military personnel. Anti-mine campaigners could consistently trump military experts by pointing to the clear disjuncture between mine warfare theory and practice.[46]

This is an important observation. Transnational civil society continues to have a significant influence on the operation of the Mine Ban Convention because of this. And its research on the anti-personnel mine problem and its effects, through publications such as the annual *Landmine Monitor* published by the International Campaign to Ban Landmines, adds credibility to its views.[47] Similar civil society attempts at empirical data collection have begun both on small arms, explosive remnants of war and, in particular, cluster munitions because of their deleterious humanitarian effects.

It is no coincidence that the international humanitarian mine action community was also at the forefront of successful subsequent efforts in the CCW process in Geneva to develop international rules on alleviating the effects of explosive remnants of war.[48] Once again this drew upon the experience of practitioners in the post-conflict humanitarian field, which helped to keep political realities aligned with facts on the ground in humanitarian and military terms, as well with public expectations.

Humanitarian approaches and human security concepts have made far fewer inroads in the context of multilateral processes aimed at curbing so-called weapons of mass destruction. Nuclear, chemical and biological chemical weapons programmes have always been the subjects of particular secrecy for governments and can be central to their notions of national survival and prestige. Moreover, although their use has not been unprecedented, it has been sufficiently rare to make it difficult for a comprehensive survey of their humanitarian effects to be developed by open-source means. First-hand technical knowledge has always been difficult to divulge for reasons of state security, as the Mordechai Vanunu case in Israel showed.[49] (At the forefront of the antipersonnel mine ban campaign, by contrast, were former military engineers turned humanitarian deminers.) In the mine ban campaign, and to some lesser extent in the context of explosive remnants and even illicit trade in small arms and light weapons, mutual trust has evolved between civil society campaigners and government negotiators. A greater divide remains where weapons of mass destruction are concerned between humanitarian and "hard" national security viewpoints that needs to be bridged by more coherent human security ideas.

This does not mean that humanitarian efforts to frame these types of disarmament challenge are not under way. The BioWeapons Prevention Project, recently established by NGOs to "report regularly on developments related to compliance of governments and other entities with the BTWC and other international treaties that codify the norm against BW", has begun reporting.[50] This civil-society initiated transparency measure may be as significant in prompting public concerns by revealing the limits of publicly available data as any new revelations it contains.

For its part the ICRC launched a public appeal in September 2002 entitled "Biotechnology, Weapons and Humanity" aimed at drawing attention to the need for prevention of hostile use of the life sciences from a humanitarian perspective. (There is a precedent for this: the ICRC launched an appeal in 1918 that helped result in the 1925 Geneva Protocol banning the use of asphyxiating gases on the battlefield.) Basing its actions on its humanitarian mandate, the ICRC has not only undertaken to work with governments but also sought to improve awareness at the individual and institutional level in the professional life sciences. The ICRC is trying to promote international and domestic laws against biological weapons, and prompt actions at the state and non-state level to translate these into effective practical action.[51]

The ICRC approach demonstrates that *bottom-up* humanitarian approaches can benefit the diplomatic disarmament and arms control domain by raising awareness of the relevant international norms and encouraging consistent action. As such, this holds practical lessons for the disarmament and arms control "community of practice" in responding to problems of complexity and individual motivations for hostile use of the life sciences. What is most distinctive about the ICRC approach is that it is derived from public health models of risk assessment and reduction—an approach that appears to resonate with the international scientific and medical communities. In particular, the ICRC stresses the need to contextualize efforts to prevent poisoning and deliberate spreading of disease within the context of broader public health and development efforts rather than simply in terms of fighting "bioterrorism". Rather than predicated solely on a national security approach, which elicits suspicion among many individuals in the professional life sciences, the ICRC *web of prevention* concept can be characterized as a distinctively humanitarian response to a proliferation challenge.

CONCLUDING COMMENT

This introductory paper has suggested some ideas about new ways in which problems associated with multilateral disarmament and arms control negotiating processes might be viewed. It has attempted to do so without leaning on the concept of "political will", because this leads us into an analytical dead end. While useful as an indicator, pointing to political will as an explanation obscures more specific, or deeper-seated, problems in terms of "getting to yes" in multilateral negotiations. "Thinking outside the box" in pursuit of more effective multilateral outcomes requires more than increasing resources or proclamations of political commitment: it requires examining the conditions under which negotiations occur, and optimizing them to respond to current challenges. Past working practices and assumptions should be regularly reviewed to check that they actually make sense in the contexts to which they are applied.

To this end an alternative has been suggested, and that is to examine the multilateral "community of practice" within which negotiators work, and the way in which this contributes to shaping the choices, for better or for worse, that negotiators make. This does not ignore the specific political parameters and political pressures that can make or break a multilateral negotiation that are, naturally, at the forefront of negotiators' minds. But it provides an apparatus for viewing these interactions as more than simply exertion of the levers of national preponderance. Such an approach is necessary because diplomats are more than simply functionaries and spokespeople for their governments. As anyone who has participated in a multilateral negotiation instinctively knows, the inherited structures and working methods of a negotiation juxtaposed with the attitudes, personal style, experience and personal judgement of its participants have a major influence in creating the conditions for success or failure, through the iterative dynamics that develop.

Another theme of this article is that increasing complexity and interconnectedness are creating new challenges for traditional ways of looking at the world and responses in international security terms. Multilateral negotiators are used to thinking of "progress" or deeper-seated changes in technology, geopolitics, socio-economic conditions or the environment as the backdrop to their play. But, as examples used here indicate (including small arms and light weapons and developments in the life sciences), complex feedback processes involving individual and other non-state behaviour make risks and responses increasingly tricky to frame adequately for the purposes of problem-solving. Such developments are, in fact, not a backdrop to multilateral processes but the equivalent of a stage floor—a floor that is continually moving. At the very least, new props are going to be needed, and so is fresh dialogue.

One matrix of assumptions that needs review concerns national security, as it is traditionally regarded. Too often it is used as a trump card to prevent debate or reform of aspects of a process, such as rules of procedure or decision-making mechanisms. While it is improbable that national security prerogatives would or could be entirely discarded as a final safeguard in negotiations, diplomatic practitioners need to critique its use on a continual case-by-case basis against a broader range of concerns.

Bringing humanitarian perspectives further into multilateral disarmament and arms control's community of practice would help. Humanitarian approaches have already contributed in substantial measure to success on some conventional weapon issues, for instance in the achievement and implementation of the Mine Ban Convention. Human security concepts have been useful in conceiving how security benefits for the individual and for the community can be met, and have been grounded in reality by the involvement of the field-based humanitarian community alongside governments. Such approaches—bringing disarmament back to what it is really about in practical terms, and offering a window on understanding and capitalizing on individual and community-level behaviours—would yield benefit across the disarmament and arms control spectrum. These are desperately needed, including in "hard-core" national security areas such as nuclear and biological disarmament because preventing or diverting hostile intent is going to become more critical as technology advances and diffuses.

Viewing disarmament as humanitarian action will not be without its costs. Greater non-state actor input into disarmament and arms control processes—like the Conference on Disarmament, or the NPT, for instance, in which such input is currently highly circumscribed—may make some states uncomfortable. But inviting a broader range of input, whether it be humanitarian mine clearance operators in the Mine Ban Convention or physicians and civil nuclear scientists in the NPT, should not be seen as some sort of favour to transnational civil society. In fact, a richer flow of information and of knowledgeable perspectives is a practical means to making multilateral processes more effective, especially if they lead to questioning features that have lost their purpose and utility. Failure to do so will foreclose options for multilateral effectiveness to improve and, as a consequence, likely undermine states' own security.

Human security or broader humanitarian approaches to disarmament and arms control are not "one size fits all" solutions to multilateral problem-solving. Obviously they are context dependent, but a key characteristic— the involvement of those they are intended to help and those who carry out or live with the realities of work on the ground within a coherent and goal (rather than process) oriented framework—is relevant in any context. One main benefit, in combination with examining negotiation activities in the context of a community of practice, is that it should help multilateral practitioners to choose and, if need be, devise appropriate methods and objectives.

For multilateral effectiveness of disarmament and arms control processes to improve, practitioners must be more willing to be critical of their working methods and behaviours—not all of which persist for sound reasons—and to discard or modify them more readily. The most painful part of such a process may be the point at which respective governments and their negotiating representatives realize that abandoning or transforming old postures or practices will concede a specific advantage. But there is more to be gained than lost from this in the longer run; that is, *if* falling back on crutch explanations like "that's the way it's always been done" or "lack of political will" can be avoided. What is there to lose in a contemporary multilateral disarmament environment beset by stagnation and lack of ambition?

Notes

1   Multilateralism as meant here: a commitment to maximum participation in dialogue among political, social, economic and cultural forces as a means of resolving conflicts and designing institutional processes. See R. Cox, *Program on Multilateralism and the United Nations System, 1990-1995*, Tokyo: United Nations University, April 1991, p. 4.

2   See United Nations, *Report of the Secretary-General's High Level Panel on Threats, Challenges and Change—A More Secure World: Our Shared Responsibility*, New York: United Nations, 2004. This report can be downloaded from: http://www.un.org/secureworld/.

3   See Chapter 2 ("New Dimensions of Human Security") in *UNDP Human Development Report 1994*, New York: United Nations Development Programme, 1994, pp. 22-46.

4   Convention on the Prohibition of the Use, Stockpiling, Production and Transfer of Anti-Personnel Mines and on Their Destruction of 18 September 1997, Protocol on Explosive Remnants of War of 28 November 2003 (Protocol V to the Convention on Prohibitions or Restrictions on the Use of Certain Conventional Weapons Which May Be Deemed to Be Excessively Injurious or to Have Indiscriminate Effects of 10 October 1980), United Nations Programme of Action to Prevent, Combat and Eradicate the Illicit Trade in Small Arms and Light Weapons in All Its Aspects (A/CONF.192/15), 20 July 2001. The small arms programme of action was drafted as a political document and is not legally binding on states.

5   Robert J. Mathews and Timothy L. H. McCormack, "The Influences of Humanitarian Principles in the Negotiation of Arms Control Treaties", *International Review of the Red Cross*, Vol. 81, No. 834, June 1999, pp. 331-352, p. 333.

6   The 1968 Nuclear Non-Proliferation Treaty (NPT), for example, explicitly created two categories of State, with the intention of preventing the spread of nuclear weapons. Five countries (China, France, the Soviet Union, the United Kingdom and the United States) were granted status as "nuclear-weapon states", although Article 6 of the Treaty obligates them to eliminating eventually their nuclear-weapon arsenals. The NPT commits its other members ("non-nuclear-weapon states") to forego the right to develop or possess these weapons. See Jozef Goldblat, *Arms Control: the New Guide to Negotiations and Agreements*, 2nd edition, PRIO/SIPRI, London: Sage Books, 2002, pp. 101-109.

7   Centre for Humanitarian Dialogue, *Report of the 3rd Humanitarian Negotiators' Network Annual Meeting—Contextual Considerations*, Talloire, 12-14 May 2003, p. 3, http:www.hdcentre.org.

8   For a comprehensive survey see Adam Roberts and Richard Guelff, *Documents on the Laws of War*, 3rd edition, Oxford/New York: Oxford University Press, 2000.

9   Jozef Goldblat, *Agreements for Arms Control—a Critical Survey*, Stockholm: Stockholm International Peace Research Institute, 1982, p. 89.

10 Mathews and McCormack, op. cit., p. 333.

11 This withstanding, there are differing views over the effectiveness of these norm-building paradigms. Criticism of multilateral disarmament and arms control is not difficult to find, and this paper cites a number of examples. In the IHL field Jochnick and Normand have argued, for example, that "in both World Wars the laws of war played analogous roles. In each conflict the law served as a powerful rhetorical device to reassure anxious publics that the conflict would be confined within just limitations … [and was] subverted to the dictates of battle, reduced to a propaganda battlefield where belligerents traded attacks and counter-attacks". See Chris af Jochnick and Roger Normand, "The Legitimation of Violence: A Critical History of the Laws of War", *Harvard International Law Journal*, Vol. 35, No. 1, Winter 1994, pp. 49-95.

12 United Nations Security Council Resolution S/RES/1540 of 28 April 2004, operative paragraph 4.

13 Statement by United States Under-Secretary of State, John Bolton, *Stopping the Spread of Weapons of Mass Destruction in the Asian-Pacific Region: the Role of the Proliferation Security Initiative*, Tokyo American Centre, Japan, 27 October 2004, p. 1.

14 Ibid., p. 2.

15 Andrew Prosser and Herbert Schoville Jr., *The Proliferation Security Initiative in Perspective*, 16 June 2004, http://www.cdi.org.

16 For useful and concise arguments in favour of multilateral engagement—written with a view to the United States after the attacks of September 2001—see Shepard Forman, Princeton Lyman and Stewart Patrick, "The United States in a Global Age: The Case for Multilateral Engagement", *Paying for Essentials: A Policy Paper Series*, New York: New York University Center on International Cooperation, May 2002. Despite this focus on the United States, the paper is of more general relevance in arguments for the engagement of powerful states in multilateral processes.

17 *Report of the Secretary-General's High-Level Panel on Threats, Challenges and Change*, pp. 1-5.

18 For instance, see United States Assistant Secretary of State Stephen G. Rademaker's statement to the Conference on Disarmament, "The Commitment of the United States to Effective Multilateralism",

13 February 2003, Geneva, Switzerland, p. 2. "On behalf of my government ... I reject any suggestion that the United States is not committed to multilateral means of achieving policy goals. To the contrary, properly understood, our policies are profoundly multilateralist. If current US policy differs at all from US policy in the past, it is a result of our recognition that, in the post-Cold War era, multilateralism is more important than ever, and that without leadership—without backbone—multilateralism is predictably condemned to failure. In a number of recent instances where we thought it necessary, we have chosen to provide the leadership—the backbone—required for multilateralism to succeed. Our insistence that multilateralism be effective may not always make us popular, but it hardly makes us 'unilateralist'".

More recently President Bush's new appointment as Secretary of State, Dr Condoleeza Rice, declared in her Senate confirmation hearing: "We must use American diplomacy to help create a balance of power in the world that favours freedom. And the time for diplomacy is now." See excerpts from this statement at: http://news.bbc.co.uk/go/pr/fr/-/1/hi/world/americas/4184751.stm.

[19] Forman, Lyman and Patrick, op. cit., p. 15.

[20] See Chapter 4 in this volume by Vanessa Martin Randin and John Borrie, "A Comparison Between Arms Control and Other Multilateral Negotiation Processes".

[21] Ron Scollon, *Mediated Discourse as Social Interaction: A Study of News Discourse,* Boston: Addison Wesley, 1998, pp. 12-13.

[22] The author would include the modern life sciences in this description of the information sciences. Molecular structures, including genes are, after all, repositories for information in organic form. Many advances in biotechnology, for instance, involve the interpreting and—in some cases—the modifying of this information.

[23] See Chapter 6, "After the Smoke Clears: Assessing the Effects of Small Arms Availability" in *Small Arms Survey 2001: Profiling the Problem,* Oxford: Oxford University Press, 2001, pp. 197-249.

[24] The term "national security" was apparently first used by United States Secretary of Defense James Forrestal at United States Senate hearings on the post-Second World War American defence policy and military structure. See Keith Krause, "Is Human Security More than Just a Good Idea?" in *Promoting Security: But How and For Whom?—Contributions to BICC's Ten-year Anniversary Conference,* Bonn International Centre

for Conversion (BICC) Brief 30, Bonn: BICC, October 2004, pp. 43-46, p. 43.

[25] For a brief (and classic) analysis of this trend see Michael Howard, *War in European History*, Oxford Paperbacks, New York: Oxford University Press, 1976.

[26] See John G. Stoessinger, *The Might of Nations: World Politics in Our Time*, 9th ed., New York: McGraw-Hill, 1990, pp. 227-238.

[27] See Tobias Debiel, "The Need for an Integrated Security Concept" in BICC, op. cit., pp. 52-55, p. 52.

[28] See Martin Griffiths, *Fifty Key Thinkers in International Relations*, London: Routledge, 1999, for an overview. The additional examples mentioned here are: Michael Ignatieff, *Empire-Lite: Nation-Building in Bosnia, Kosovo, Afghanistan*, London: Vintage, 2003; Robert Kagan, *Paradise and Power: America and Europe in the New World Order*, New York: Atlantic Books, 2003; and Samuel Huntington, *The Clash of Civilizations and the Remaking of World Order*, New York: Touchstone/Simon & Schuster, 1996.

[29] For further background on some of these negotiations see April Carter, *Success and Failure in Arms Control Negotiations*, Stockholm International Peace Research Institute, Stockholm: Oxford University Press/SIPRI, 1989; and Jozef Goldblat, *Arms Control: The New Guide to Negotiations and Agreements*, 2nd ed., PRIO/SIPRI, London: Sage Publications, 2002.

[30] Key to implementation of the BTWC prohibitions is the so-called "general purpose criterion" contained within Articles I and III of this treaty, intended to "future-proof" it against future advances in the life sciences and ensure that they fall within the Convention's purview. For more detail on the "general purpose criterion" of the BTWC see "Non-Lethal' Weapons, the CWC and the BWC" in *The Harvard-Sussex CBW Conventions Bulletin*, Issue 61, September 2003, pp. 1-2.

[31] Emergence refers to a process by which a system of interacting sub-units acquires qualitatively new properties that cannot be understood as the simple addition of their individual contributions. These system-level properties arise unexpectedly from non-linear interactions among a system's components. For more background see Steven Johnson, *Emergence*, London: Penguin, 2001.

[32] Professor Malcolm Dando, "Statement to the Commission of the 28th Conference of the Red Cross and Red Crescent Movement on Biotechnology, Weapons and Humanity", Geneva, 4 December 2003, p. 2, http://www.scienceforhumanity.org.

33 For instance, the polio virus was recreated synthetically and reported in 2002. See Jeronimo Cello, Aniko V. Pail, Eckard Wimmer, "Chemical Synthesis of Poliovirus cDNA: Generation of Infectious Virus in the Absence of Nature Template" in *Science*, Vol. 297, 9 August 2002, pp. 1016-1018. Moreover, researchers in the United States reported in early 2005 an "unexpectedly sudden advance in synthesizing long lengths of DNA [which puts] researchers within reach of manufacturing genomes the size of the smallpox virus. See Nicholas Wade, "Synthetic Virus in Reach", *International Herald Tribune/The New York Times*, 12 January 2005.

34 See "The Journey of the Sorcerer" in *The Economist: Technology Quarterly*, 4-10 December 2004, pp. 27-28.

35 See BBC News, "A Glimpse Inside the Virus Writer", <http://news.bbc.co.uk/go/pr/fr/-/2/hi/technology/3240901.stm> (5 November 2003).

36 *Small Arms Survey...*, op. cit., p. 234.

37 Robert Muggah and Peter Batchelor, *"Development Held Hostage": Assessing the Effects of Small Arms on Human Development—A Preliminary Study of the Socio-Economic Impacts and Development Linkages of Small Arms Proliferation, Availability and Use*, New York: United Nations Development Programme, April 2002, p. 3, http://www.undp.org/erd/smallarms.

38 See the special section by various authors entitled "What is 'Human Security'" in *Security Dialogue*, Vol. 35, No. 3, September 2004, pp. 345-372.

39 United Nations Development Programme, *Human Development Report 1994*, New York: UNDP, 1994, p. 22.

40 Muggah and Batchelor, op. cit., p. 12.

41 See the Independent Commission on Human Security, *Human Security Now: Report of the Commission on Human Security*, New York: Commission on Human Security, 2003, p. 12. The Commission frames human security in the following way: "to protect the vital core of all human lives in ways that enhance human freedoms and human fulfilment. Human security means protecting fundamental freedoms that are the essence of life. It means protecting people from critical (severe) and pervasive (widespread) threats and situations. It means using processes that build on people's strengths and aspirations. It means creating political, social, environmental, economic, military and cultural systems that together give people the building blocks of survival, livelihood and dignity. The vital core of life is a set of

elementary rights and freedoms people enjoy. What people consider to be 'vital'—what they consider to be 'of the essence of life' and 'crucially important'—varies across individuals and societies. That is why any concept of human security must be dynamic. And that is why we refrain from proposing an itemized list of what makes up international security."

42   See Taylor Owen, "Challenges and Opportunities for Defining and Measuring Human Security" in *Disarmament Forum*, 2004/3, pp. 15-24, p. 19.

43   Ibid., p. 23.

44   See, for instance, Robin M. Coupland, "Amputations from anti-personnel mine injuries of the leg", *Annals of the Royal College of Surgeons of England*, No. 71, 1989, pp. 405-408, Robin Coupland and A. Korver, "Injuries from anti-personnel mines: the experience of the ICRC", *British Medical Journal*, No. 303, 1991, pp. 1509-1512 and Rae McGrath and Eric Stover, "Injuries from Landmines", *British Medical Journal*, No. 303, 1991, p. 1492.

45   See Martin Dahinden, "Humanitarian Demining at a Crossroads—A Farewell Lecture", Geneva International Centre for Humanitarian Demining (GICHD), Geneva, 1 July 2004. Dahinden was Director of GICHD and a career diplomat, http://www.gichd.ch.

46   Don Hubert, *The Landmine Ban: A Case Study in Humanitarian Advocacy*, Thomas J. Watson Jr. Institute for International Studies, Occasional Paper No. 42, Providence: Thomas J. Watson Jr. Institute for International Studies, 2000, p. 31. Hubert participated in the Antipersonnel Mine Ban Convention negotiations as a member of the Canadian delegation.

47   For downloadable copies of this annual report go to the ICBL website at http://www.icbl.org/lm.

48   Protocol on Explosive Remnants of War (see note 4 above).

49   See BBC News story, "Vanunu wanted to avert holocaust", at <http://news.bbc.co.uk/1/hi/world/middle_east/3758693.stm> (Saturday 29 May 2004, 0826 GMT 0926 UK).

50   The first (2004) edition of the BioWeapons Prevention Project's *BioWeapons Monitor* is available from the BWPP website at http://www.bwpp.org.

51   The ICRC mission is to "protect the lives and dignity of victims of war and internal violence and to provide them with assistance. It directs and coordinates the international relief activities conducted by the Movement in situations of conflict. It also endeavours to prevent

suffering by promoting and strengthening international humanitarian law and universal humanitarian principles". See the ICRC leaflet, *Biotechnology, Weapons and Humanity*, Geneva: ICRC, 2003, http://www.scienceforhumanity.org.

CHAPTER 2

MODELLING ARMED VIOLENCE:
A TOOL FOR HUMANITARIAN DIALOGUE
IN DISARMAMENT AND ARMS CONTROL

Robin M. Coupland[1]

The use of weapons with intent to cause physical harm can be analysed in terms of health because, ultimately, it affects people's physical, psychological or social well-being.[2] Analysing armed violence from a health perspective carries the advantage that it permits generic and objective consideration of the effects of armed violence on its victims—frequently a consideration driven by emotion—before entering into discussions of the legal, political or "humanitarian" issues of a particular context. This paper presents a model of armed violence and its effects on the health of the victims; it is proposed as a means to introduce a humanitarian perspective into dialogue about disarmament and arms control.[3]

MODELLING ARMED VIOLENCE AND ITS EFFECTS

When people suffer the effects of use of a particular weapon, at some previous time, the weapon has to be transferred into the hands of the user; before this it has to be produced and before production it has to be designed and developed.[4] The activities along the continuum of "design-to-production-to-transfer-to-use" are important potential determinants of the effects of armed violence. It is no coincidence that these activities are precisely those regulated in many multilateral arms control treaties. In public health terms, these determinants translate into "risk factors" for any particular impact on health of armed violence.

The fact that the effects on health of armed violence have identifiable risk factors is the basis of the model. Whatever the nature of armed violence, the risk factors for a given effect are the:

- Potential of the weapon to cause the effect (corresponding to design);
- Number of potential users armed (corresponding to production and transfer);
- Vulnerability of the victim (the potential to suffer the effect); and
- Potential for violence (intentional use of physical force).

Effects of armed violence are only generated as long as the potential of each risk factor has a positive value; each is a necessary but not sufficient cause of the effects in question. This applies to any act of armed violence with any effect in any context.

But is this model valid from a scientific point of view? Research has shown how information from real events about both effects and risk factors can be translated into meaningful data by the model. The same research has shown, in relation to deaths and injuries, that the risk factors independently influence lethality of a context.[5] This has been tested against three data sets.

Logic tells us that the risk factors interact. But how they do so is complex. The potential for violence using weapons must be influenced by the user's perceptions of the other three risk factors. In other words, the relationship between weapons and violence is played out in the psychology of the user or users. By extrapolation, the weapons themselves and their availability are major determinants of the nature, timing and extent of armed violence. Furthermore, if, from a generic perspective, one can validate the risk factors for a given effect, one can, in a specific context and with a degree of scientific validity, identify the nature of the risk factors. This has important legal implications because it may speak to the perpetrators' intent or the degree of vulnerability of victims when the truth is not forthcoming.

In terms of prevention, addressing only one risk factor may be ineffective in preventing or limiting any given effect of armed violence unless that risk factor is eliminated completely. As will be indicated in relation to chemical and biological weapons, any single preventive measure falls into one of the categories given by four risk factors. This implies that multiple preventive measures, if referable to some or all risk factors, may act in synergy.

Among other uses, the model can serve as a tool for dialogue on any issue related to weapons and armed violence. Most importantly, it forces simultaneous consideration of the victims and their vulnerabilities. Three subjects that are topical issues in the arms control arena indicate how the model could enhance a dialogue by bringing "humanitarian" concerns to centre stage. The first is the availability of small arms and light weapons; the second is so-called "non-lethal" weapons; and the third is chemical and biological weapons. The paper ends with a more philosophical view of the importance given to weapons and armed violence in human affairs and proposes that the model could help us comprehend better the notion of reasonable use of force.

SMALL ARMS AND LIGHT WEAPONS

Considering the availability of small arms and light weapons within this model means that we must first clarify what it is about this issue that concerns us. One way of expressing the effects of concern might be the number of people killed, injured or coerced with military assault rifles outside the context of armed conflict. By referring to the model, it is immediately clear that reducing the availability of such weapons is not the only measure that might prevent this effect; and further, that focusing on transfer (especially on *illicit* transfers only) is one step removed from reducing the effects. There is reason to believe that all those working on small arms issues would agree with this analysis.

Some measures may be more appropriate than others in certain contexts. These include: first, limiting the potential of the weapon to cause the effect by reducing availability of ammunition; secondly, other means to reduce the immediate availability of military rifles such as voluntary submission, forced disarmament, disarmament at demobilization, buy-back programmes, exchanges and encouraging or enforcing safe storage.[6] Means to reduce vulnerability of unarmed people include ensuring good governance, building an effective police force and preventing the failure of states.[7] Equipping police forces with handguns only (which are more appropriate for the mission of law enforcement) would lessen the chances of more powerful military rifles being used indiscriminately or with excessive force. In terms of the nature of violence itself, preventive measures range from ensuring that weapons are transferred only to recipients who are likely to respect International Humanitarian Law (IHL)[8] and human rights (a preventive measure feeding off the link between different risk factors) to insisting commanders foster discipline in their troops. The "culture of armed violence" could be addressed at a school level by educational programmes that espouse non-violence and rejection of the factors that perpetuate such a culture.

Putting these and other possible preventive measures in the framework given by the model emphasizes that no single preventive measure should dominate in every context. Taken together, different measures may act in synergy. Some working on small arms issues would take issue with this analysis but to do so must refute the model.

This model also provides a useful tool for dialogue with those who wish to belittle efforts to address this issue. When discussing the problems caused by small arms in Africa, one frequently hears a counter-argument: "Well if they don't have guns, they'll do it with machetes!" The potential of a single military rifle to cause multiple deaths is obviously much higher than a commonly available farm machete. Referring to the model shows that before hundreds of thousands of people can be killed with machetes, there needs to be: first, a very large number of people armed; secondly, they must possess a very high level of intent (driven for example by tribal hatred) and, thirdly, there must be extreme vulnerability of the victims.[9] In many cases, the extreme vulnerability necessary can be brought by coercion with rifles. The model, by forcing a focus on reality, can preclude unreasonable argument.

"NON-LETHAL" WEAPONS

It is difficult to oppose the development of new means and methods of warfare, which would lead to fewer deaths, injuries, disabilities or deprivation to civilians. However, the term "non-lethal weapons" is applied to a range of old and new weapons the use of which is, purportedly, associated with low lethality. Such weapons can be classified according to how they damage or incapacitate the human body. The following categories of weapon have been cited as having "non-lethal" capabilities: kinetic energy (rubber bullets, sponge bullets, etc.); entangling technologies (nets, sticky foam); chemical weapons; biological weapons; acoustic beams; electric shock technologies; infrasound; and electromagnetic waves of a variety of wavelengths.[10]

Lethality is an effect; it means the proportion of people affected by the use of a weapon who ultimately die.[11] The model explains how all risk factors play into lethality of a context that can theoretically range from zero to 100%. Therefore, the lethality associated with the use of a particular weapon is an outcome of context; it is not an inherent property of the weapon. This analysis shows how claiming that a weapon is "non-lethal" or even "less than lethal" does not reconcile with an understanding brought by the model. The notion has politically correct or even humanitarian connotations and is, therefore, an effective marketing strategy.

Significantly, blinding lasers were developed in the "non-lethal" paradigm but their use has nevertheless been prohibited in armed conflict.[12]

Furthermore, conventional weapons (firearms, mortars, shells, etc.) are not necessarily "lethal". In the context of armed conflict, the lethality resulting from the use of conventional weapons as recorded since the Second World War is around 20%. Conventional weapons can be used without any lethality: posturing, threats, firing away from the person are all "non-lethal" options. Other weapons lend themselves to use by, for example, police in law enforcement or riot control; their use in these circumstances can reasonably be expected to result in a low lethality. Deaths are clearly less likely when police or military bodies use tear gas or rubber bullets for law enforcement as compared with the use of firearms.

Therefore, the main question is not about the lethality of weapons. It is about whether a given weapon is appropriate for the mission while knowing the lethality and permanent injury likely to occur in the execution of that mission. This is the central issue when considering the legality of any weapons whether for law enforcement or for military use in armed conflict according to human rights law or IHL respectively. Specifically, states parties to the 1977 Protocol I Additional to the 1949 Geneva Conventions of 12 August 1949 have an obligation to review the legality of any new weapon, means or method of warfare that state is studying, developing, acquiring or adopting.[13] There is no exception for weapons deemed "non-lethal".

According to the doctrine of the North Atlantic Treaty Organisation (NATO), "non-lethal" weapons will only ever be a complement to conventional weapons.[14] One major concern, supported by examining the use of "non-lethal" weapons according to the model, is that if such weapons are used in armed conflict they could increase lethality on the battlefield by simply elevating the vulnerability of combatants to the effects of conventional weapons. It is pertinent that the 1993 Chemical Weapons Convention (CWC) specifically prohibits the use of riot control agents as a method of warfare.[15]

For those involved in disarmament negotiations relating to biological and chemical weapons, the term "non-lethal" has introduced considerable confusion. There is a small but growing body of opinion that both the 1972 Bacteriological (Biological) and Toxin Weapons Convention (BTWC) and the CWC will need to be revised to permit the development, production, transfer and use of "non-lethal" biological or chemical weapons. However, as with conventional weapons, use of traditional biological or chemical weapons does not necessarily lead to one hundred per cent lethality. The International Committee of the Red Cross (ICRC) is totally opposed to permitting the use of *any* chemical or biological weapons, whatever their mode of action or "lethality", as a means of warfare. This would simply be letting poisoning or deliberate spread of infectious disease back onto the battlefield.

Sun Tzu said: "Those who are not thoroughly aware of the disadvantages in the use of arms cannot be thoroughly aware of the advantages in the use of arms."[16] Unfortunately, the proponents of "non-lethal" weapons give little consideration to the disadvantages.

CHEMICAL AND BIOLOGICAL WEAPONS

Use of chemical weapons has been rare; the use of biological weapons even rarer. But advances in life sciences and biotechnology may bring in an era that sees the use of new biological or chemical weapons. Some of these would conceivably fulfil the definitions of both biological and chemical agents given in the BTWC and the CWC respectively. New agents could be more easily designed, more specific in their effects or more difficult to detect. New ways to deliver "traditional" and new agents could be found in parallel with the means to overcome the targets' natural or acquired defences. The user could carry out an attack in greater safety. In brief, many of the recognized disadvantages of chemical or biological weapons could be eliminated; new biological or chemical weapons would then become a much more attractive option for anyone contemplating their use.

Approaching chemical and biological weapons with the model in mind forces us to think what this is really all about: it is about minimizing the chances of people suffering poisoning and the deliberate spread of disease. Because the model incorporates the fact that the design and development of weapons, their production, their transfer and their use are prerequisites for victims suffering the effects, it is an appropriate tool for untangling the complexities of preventing the use of chemical or biological weapons.

Any single measure that might prevent poisoning and deliberate spread of infectious disease is referable to one or more of the risk factors. Examples are: how public health preparedness reduces *vulnerability*; the total prohibition and, at a national level, criminalization of poisoning and deliberate spread of disease aims to eliminate *use*; inspections, intelligence and customs regulations impact on *production* and *transfer* to would-be perpetrators; promoting notions of responsibility among scientists would address *design* and *development*. These measures overlap and integrate with states' obligations under the BTWC and the CWC. It becomes obvious how each preventive measure is necessary but not in itself sufficient to minimize the risk of poisoning and the deliberate spread of infectious disease. This approach provides the basis for what the ICRC is promoting as the "web of prevention".[17] Practical aspects of this are communicated in a series of imperatives: recognize the risks! Maximize what you can do in your domain to reduce the risks! Listen to what others are doing! Coordinate your thinking and action!

The model serves to emphasize that minimizing the risks of the advances in life sciences and biotechnology being used for poisoning and deliberate spread of infectious disease is, by necessity, a multidisciplinary and collaborative endeavour.

REASONABLE USE OF FORCE

The majority of international news reports refer to acts of armed violence, threats of armed violence, effects of armed violence, agreements that restrain the capacity for armed violence or means of inflicting armed violence. It is obvious that armed violence and its effects are very much in our collective conscience and determine how international affairs are played out. Anthropologists and historians argue that human cultures and a world built on the notion of the nation state are born of acts of armed violence, the capacity to inflict armed violence and agreements, which restrain this capacity.[18] In other words, armed violence has always carried a fundamental importance for human existence because the basis of group defence or law enforcement is ultimately about how individuals or groups apply force to each other or threaten each other. This is why most societies recognize that certain of their members should carry weapons legitimately. Whilst this baseline view of militarism and law enforcement by police may appear simplistic, it is safe to say that armed violence and its regulation are somehow profoundly implicated in how all humans live and interact. This is why restraining armed violence and reasonable use of force constitutes the central underpinnings of the United Nations Charter, IHL and human rights.

The model permits a more objective and consistent way to judge whether an act of armed violence is consistent with the notion of reasonable use of force. Whether the victims of the use of a weapon are criminals, rioters, citizens expressing their right to free speech or enemy soldiers, the following series of questions must be answered: given the actual or predicted effects of any form of armed violence, is the type of weapon appropriate for the context? Is the weapon deployed in an appropriate number? Have the victims'—or potential victims'—vulnerabilities been taken into account? Is the use restrained—and if so, how?

It becomes obvious that not only ameliorating the effects of armed violence but also restraining the capacity for armed violence are profoundly linked to a positive and collective human existence.[19] Do not notions of humanity also become relevant here? If the fundamental importance to humanity of armed violence is recognized, referring to the model could have profound implications for how affairs are conducted in the international sphere and how international law, in particular, the United Nations Charter, the international law of arms control and disarmament, IHL and human rights law are developed and applied. Such assertions may seem far removed from the subject of this paper but, at the end of the day, from a public health perspective, these bodies of international law serve primarily to manage armed violence.

CONCLUSION

The model of armed violence presented here takes into account the effects of armed violence and pertinent risk factors. The examples given show how understanding this model could provide powerful tools for dialogue in the domain of disarmament and arms control. But is it "humanitarian" dialogue?

This model permits a consistent and "evidence-based" dialogue about the victims of armed violence and their vulnerabilities. International *humanitarian* law is about protection of victims of armed violence and their vulnerabilities. It follows that this model provides a means (and possibly the only means) to bring a humanitarian dialogue to disarmament and arms control precisely because it provides a consistent and "evidence-based" dialogue about the victims of armed violence and their vulnerabilities.

Notes

1   The opinions expressed in this paper are the author's own. They do not represent the views or policy of the ICRC.

2   Definition of violence: the intentional use of physical force or power threatened or actual, against oneself, another person, or against a group or community, that either results in or has a likelihood to result in injury, death, psychological harm, mal-development or deprivation (see J. P. Koplan, M. Rosenberg, E. Krug, *Violence prevention: A public health policy*, Atlanta: Centers for Disease Control and Prevention, 1998. Definition of health: a state of complete physical, mental and social well-being and not merely the absence of disease (World Health Organization, *Preamble to the Constitution of the World Health Organization*, as adopted by the International Health Conference, New York, 19-22 June 1946); a weapon is a material thing designed or used or usable as an instrument for inflicting bodily harm (*Oxford English Dictionary*, 2nd edition, Oxford: Clarendon Press, 1989.

3   R. M. Coupland, "Armed Violence", *Medicine and Global Survival*, Vol. 7, 2001, pp. 33-37.

4   Ibid., "The Effects of Weapons on Health", *The Lancet*, Vol. 347, 1996, pp. 450-451.

5   N. Taback and R. Coupland, "Towards Collation and Modelling of the Global Cost of Armed Violence on Civilians", *Medicine, Conflict and Survival*, Vol. 21, 2005, pp. 19-27.

6   Small Arms Survey, *Small Arms Survey 2004: Rights at Risk*, Oxford: Oxford University Press, 2004.

7   ICRC/Programme for Strategic and International Security Studies (PSIS), *State Collapse and Reconstruction: Lessons and Strategies*, report of a conference held under the auspices of the ICRC and PSIS, Geneva, 7-9 December 2000.

8   ICRC, *Arms Availability and the Situation of Civilians in Armed Conflict*, Geneva: ICRC, 1999.

9   D. Grossman, *On Killing: The Psychological Cost of Learning to Kill in War and Society*, Boston: Little Brown and Co, 1995, pp. 97-137.

10   National Research Council of the National Academies of Science, *An Assessment of Non-Lethal Weapons Science and Technology*, Washington, DC: The National Academies Press, 2003.

11   R. Coupland and D. Loye, "Legal and Health Issues: International Humanitarian Law and Lethality or Non-Lethality of Weapons", *Non-Lethal Weapons*, London: Jane's Information Group, 2000, pp. 60-66.

12   Protocol IV of the Convention on Prohibitions or Restrictions on the Use of Certain Conventional Weapons Which May Be Deemed to Be Excessively Injurious or to Have Indiscriminate Effects.

13   Protocol I Additional to the Geneva Conventions of 12 August 1949, and relating to the Protection of Victims of International Armed Conflicts (Protocol I), adopted on 8 June 1977, Article 36, which states: "In the study, development, acquisition or adoption of a new weapon, means or method of warfare, a High Contracting Party is under an obligation to determine whether its employment would, in some or all circumstances, be prohibited by this Protocol or by any other rule of international law applicable to the High Contracting Party."

14   NATO, "NATO Policy on Non-Lethal Weapons", *NATO Press Statement*, Brussels, 13 October 1999.

15   1993 Chemical Weapons Convention, Article 1.5.

16   S. Tzu, *The Art of War*, Boston: Shambala, 1988.

17   For more information on the ICRC initiative on Biotechnology, Weapons and Humanity, see www.scienceforhumanity.org.

18   For more information see J. Keegan, *A History of Warfare*, London: Pimlico, 1994, pp. 386-393; N. A. Chagnon, "Life Histories, Blood Revenge and Warfare in a Tribal Population", *Science*, Vol. 239, 1988, pp. 985-992; J. Diamond, *Guns, Germs and Steel: A Short History of*

Everybody for the Last 13,000 Years, London: Vintage, 1998; J. Glover, *Humanity: A Moral History of the Twentieth Century*, London: Jonathan Cape, 1999.

[19] R. Coupland, "The Humanity of Humans: Philosophy, Science, Health or Rights?", *Health and Human Rights*, Vol. 7, No. 1, 2003, pp. 159-166.

CHAPTER 3

DECONSTRUCTING DISARMAMENT: THE CHALLENGE OF MAKING THE DISARMAMENT AND ARMS CONTROL MACHINERY RESPONSIVE TO THE HUMANITARIAN IMPERATIVE

Patrick McCarthy[1]

INTRODUCTION[2]

This paper outlines how existing disarmament and arms control structures and procedures enable and constrain the international community in its efforts to meet common security challenges. It points to how these security challenges are beginning to be defined in a different way—with a much stronger focus on what this paper will call the "humanitarian imperative"—and the problems that this poses for the standard operating procedures of disarmament and arms control inherited from the Cold War era. The paper takes as its starting point a revolutionary and very controversial idea from philosophy—Derrida's concept of deconstructionism—and applies it to a preliminary examination of the practice of disarmament and arms control. It argues that the structures, procedures and institutions that the international community employs to address common security challenges matter for two reasons. First, they influence whether or not multilateral agreements are reached. Secondly, they influence the effectiveness of these agreements.

DERRIDA AND DECONSTRUCTIONISM

The Algerian-born French philosopher, Jacques Derrida, died on 9 October 2004 at the age of 74. He was one of the most celebrated, controversial and difficult philosophers of the late twentieth century. He founded the school of thought known as "deconstructionism", whose core argument is essentially that it is impossible for the human will to be expressed accurately because of the constraints imposed upon us by the means we have of expressing it—language, of course, being one of the principal means. In other words, using the analogy of a film projector, it is impossible for human beings to project their will accurately because a distortion occurs when it is passed through the lens of language. If this idea is true, then it follows that the human will cannot be known with any certainty because we simply do not have adequate means to make it known.

Derrida spent his life examining—or "deconstructing"—written texts in a search for hidden, alternative meanings.[3] But his approach also spread to other areas of the arts and social sciences, including linguistics, anthropology and political science. The deconstructionist idea even led some architects to abandon the straight-edge, right-angle strictures of traditional architecture in order to express themselves through more amorphously shaped spaces. A striking example of the deconstructionist idea applied to architecture is the Guggenheim Museum in Bilbao, designed by Frank Gehry.

While deconstructionist thought has been applied to the study of political science and international relations theory through the development of "post-structuralist" (or "critical") schools of thought, it has not, at least to my knowledge, been applied directly to the realm of disarmament and arms control practice. So, in the spirit of an explorer gingerly stepping into uncharted territory this paper attempts, in a very preliminary manner, to offer some thoughts on why Derrida's idea may be relevant to thinking about problems in multilateral disarmament diplomacy.

APPLYING DERRIDA TO DISARMAMENT

A simple translation of Derrida's idea into the language of disarmament and arms control could read as follows:

It can be difficult for states to arrive at cooperative solutions to new security challenges because of the constraints imposed upon them by the structure of traditional disarmament diplomacy.

Before pursuing this idea further, it is first necessary to make some general observations about the role of "political will" and of the individual negotiator in disarmament diplomacy today.

THE ROLE OF POLITICAL WILL

Derrida's idea assumes that a person possesses a "will" that they would like to express. While this assumption may work at the level of the individual, it certainly does not work at the level of the international community, where it is not always the case that the "political will" exists to deal cooperatively with common security challenges.[4]

This is an important distinction. But it does not necessarily lead to the commonly-reached conclusion that if the political will to deal with a specific threat to international peace and security does not exist, then it does not really matter what kind of machinery is in place for dealing with it. This conclusion is misleading because it only takes into consideration the role that the disarmament machinery plays in allowing an existing political will to express itself. It ignores the potential role that this machinery could play, if properly designed and maintained, in actually helping to generate political will.

Political will does not just either "exist" or "not exist". It is created; usually in a painstaking manner and over a long period of time, and usually as a result of the interaction among an array of actors including governments, international organizations, non-governmental organizations (NGOs), the mass media, and global public opinion. What the international community needs, in essence, is a well-tuned and oiled multilateral disarmament machine that is not only capable of expressing the will of the international community—through treaties or other agreements—where such a will exists, but is also capable of generating political will on specific issues where it does not yet exist. The international community needs this for the same reason that human beings need a well-developed and nuanced language not only to express—through writing or speaking—ideas that we already have, but also to help us formulate ideas at which we have not yet arrived.

THE ROLE OF THE INDIVIDUAL DISARMAMENT NEGOTIATOR

A second general observation concerns the role played in multilateral disarmament diplomacy by individual disarmament negotiators. It is often assumed that these individuals are passive agents of the states they represent, unthinkingly implementing policy flowing from their capitals, through them, into the negotiating process. In fact, disarmament negotiators play a significantly greater role than this (or, at least, have the potential to do so).

Governments differ a great deal with regard to the degree of leeway they allow their disarmament diplomats, with those from larger and more powerful countries (and, therefore, bureaucracies) usually enjoying less room for manoeuvre than those from smaller states. Nevertheless, there are a number of examples in the practice of disarmament and arms control, as well as in other areas of multilateral negotiation, of individual diplomats taking initiatives during a negotiating process that feed back to modify the policy coming out of their capitals.[5] Recent advances in mobile telecommunications also allow for more immediate and regular contact between negotiators and capitals, thereby increasing the volume of information shared and, with it, the possibility of influencing policy.

Far from being passive messengers of national policy, then, individual disarmament diplomats have the potential to be active agents in the national policy-making process and thereby can also be active agents in defining the "will" of the international community.

"TRADITIONAL" VERSUS "NEW" APPROACHES TO DISARMAMENT AND ARMS CONTROL

The central argument of deconstructionism is that existing structures—be they in linguistics, archaeology or other areas—may allow us to achieve certain things while also constraining us in other important ways. This is certainly the case when it comes to states cooperating with one another to address challenges to international peace and security through disarmament and arms control. The existing disarmament machinery has certainly produced some very important treaties. The Conference on Disarmament (CD) and its precursors[6] alone, for example, have generated the Nuclear Non-Proliferation Treaty (1968), the Bacteriological (Biological) and Toxin Weapons Convention (1972), the Chemical Weapons Convention (1993), and the Comprehensive Nuclear-Test-Ban Treaty (1996).[7] But while allowing us to achieve certain things, existing structures such as the CD may also be a constraining factor in addressing some of the peace and security challenges at the top of today's international agenda.

This is the case because the ways in which the international community defines and addresses common security challenges today differs in some important respects from the ways in which such challenges were defined and addressed during the Cold War era. This paper makes a distinction between these by calling one "traditional" and the other "new" approaches to multilateral security and disarmament. The following three differences between these approaches stand out in particular:[8]

STATE SECURITY VERSUS HUMAN SECURITY

The state is still the fundamental building block of the international political system in which we live. However, the authority of the state is being undermined more and more by an ever-increasing array of factors— including globalization, the mobility of capital, the ceding of sovereignty to supranational bodies, and the emergence of non-state actors as major players on the international stage.

The very concept of state "sovereignty" is also being redefined in a way reminiscent of how the seventeenth century philosopher, Thomas Hobbes, argued that the absolute power of the "sovereign" (the King) did not derive from God, but rather from the people.[9] The echoes of this argument today assert that the sovereignty of the state is not absolute, but rather kept in existence by a state's ability to provide for the general welfare of its citizens. While the purpose of Hobbes' argument was to make the King more accountable to his subjects (while not discounting the need for a King), the argument today seeks to make the state more accountable to the international community for the way in which it treats its citizens (while not discounting the need for the state).

The continuing debate around the theory and practice of "humanitarian intervention" is just one manifestation of the way in which the concept of state sovereignty is being redefined. Another is the conclusion of the International Commission on Intervention and State Sovereignty that states have a "responsibility to protect" their citizens that, if ignored, is transferred to the broader community of states.[10] This idea has been endorsed by the United Nations Secretary-General's High-Level Panel on Threats, Challenges, and Change[11] and is likely to be further consolidated in the near future.

Similarly, while traditional approaches to arms control and disarmament tend to frame the issues in terms of threats to states, new approaches tend to be more concerned with the security and well-being of people living within states. This signals a shift in emphasis from state and military security to human and economic security. The result is a disarmament and arms control agenda that is more attuned to addressing the problem of arms and conflict in the developing world and less dominated by concerns about conventional or nuclear military confrontation in the developed world. In sum, new approaches put a stronger emphasis on the "humanitarian imperative" of disarmament and arms control.

Proof of this can be seen in recent efforts at multilateral arms control where governments are taking action to ban, regulate or clear up weapons that kill hundreds of thousands of civilians each year, predominantly in the developing world. Such weapons include anti-personnel and anti-vehicle mines, small arms and light weapons, and munitions that have been abandoned or which failed to function as intended (cumulatively referred to as explosive remnants of war).

EXCLUSIVE VERSUS INCLUSIVE NEGOTIATING PROCESSES

There are also marked differences between traditional and new approaches when it comes to the extent to which civil society groups are allowed to participate in disarmament and arms control processes. On the one hand, traditional approaches—characterized, for example, by the Nuclear Non-Proliferation Treaty and Comprehensive Nuclear-Test-Ban Treaty negotiations—have tended to be monopolized by states, with negotiations dominated by diplomats, military experts, and select groups of scientific and technical experts. Traditional approaches have also tended to lack transparency. Those participating in them have often held a virtual monopoly of both technical knowledge and the details of the negotiations themselves. Civil society groups, to the extent that they were involved at all, were typically viewed with suspicion and considered to be outsiders whose activities were to be monitored and, when necessary, curtailed.

New approaches, on the other hand, and especially those dealing with disarmament issues of particular humanitarian concern, tend to be more inclusive and more open to viewing civil society groups as the possessors and purveyors of expertise, field experience and energy potentially beneficial to multilateral negotiating processes. NGOs are now much more involved than before in the identification of problem issues, in setting the international agenda for addressing them and, in some cases at least, in helping the process along by providing expert input to multilateral negotiations. One well-known example of this is the prominent role played by NGOs during the 1990s in putting the issue of anti-personnel landmines on the international agenda and in helping negotiate a multilateral treaty to ban them. A less well-known example is the impressive leadership role played by NGOs from the late 1990s in pressuring governments to agree on a mechanism to curb the trade in so-called "conflict diamonds" that perpetuates violent conflict and fuels the demand for weapons in many parts of Africa.[12]

BUREAUCRATIC VERSUS FLEXIBLE APPROACHES

Traditional approaches to disarmament and arms control have tended to be bureaucratic, cumbersome and time-consuming. Negotiations on Mutual and Balanced Force Reductions in Europe during the Cold War era, for example, dragged on for over 15 years (1973-1989) without agreement. Initial negotiations to end nuclear testing began in 1958 but the ensuing Comprehensive Nuclear-Test-Ban Treaty has not yet entered into force. Although it continues to meet regularly, the Conference on Disarmament in Geneva has been inactive for eight years.

New approaches, on the other hand, tend to put more emphasis on speed, innovation and flexibility. The successful conclusion of the 1997 Antipersonnel Mine Ban Convention, for example, was a quick and innovative response to disappointing progress on this issue within the framework of the Convention on Certain Conventional Weapons. The United Nations Programme of Action to Prevent, Combat and Eradicate the Illicit Trade in Small Arms and Light Weapons in All Its Aspects—although not a legally binding instrument—was agreed within six years of the first United Nations General Assembly resolution on the proliferation and misuse of these weapons.[13] Likewise, the Kimberly Process—a global scheme to prevent the trade in conflict diamonds (and thus reduce conflict and the demand for weapons)—was agreed just four years after the issue first appeared on the international agenda. Significantly, multilateral action on all of these issues—anti-personnel landmines, small arms and light weapons, and conflict diamonds—was spurred and supported by intensive awareness-raising and advocacy campaigns carried out by NGOs.

PRINCIPAL CONSTRAINTS ON EXISTING MULTILATERAL DISARMAMENT MACHINERY

On the one hand, therefore, the way in which the international community identifies and addresses security challenges is changing in quite a fundamental way, reflecting a greater emphasis on human security and humanitarian concerns. On the other hand, however, the machinery and standard operating procedures that the international community has at its disposal for dealing with these challenges date, to a large extent, from the more traditional Cold War era of arms control and disarmament. This disconnection between the issues being addressed and the means available to address them imposes some important constraints on multilateral efforts to respond to today's common security challenges. The following principal constraints of the existing disarmament machinery stand out in particular:

IDENTIFYING NEW AND EMERGING SECURITY CHALLENGES

Existing multilateral disarmament machinery does not include adequate means for states, civil society and experts from specialized international organizations together to identify new and emerging threats to international peace and security in its broadest sense. Such a mechanism could facilitate the early identification of emerging threats and the formulation of multilateral responses to them.

The United Nations Secretary-General's Advisory Board on Disarmament Matters does fulfil this role to some degree, since it is composed of representatives of both governments and non-governmental bodies and interacts with civil society organizations in carrying out its work. The United Nations Institute for Disarmament Research (UNIDIR) also plays an important role by conducting research on new and emerging issues in security, disarmament and arms control. But more needs to be done to develop an inclusive mechanism for identifying common future challenges. The appointment by the United Nations Secretary-General in 2003 of a

High-level Panel on Threats, Challenges and Change is evidence that such a need exists.

SEEING DISARMAMENT AS HUMANITARIAN ACTION

Although civil society participation in multilateral disarmament and arms control processes has increased in general terms over the last few decades, it has done so quite unevenly across different issue areas. Moreover, newer processes have tended to be more open to civil society participation than older ones, which have tended to stick to established rules of procedure that exclude, or at least severely limit, non-governmental influences.

The newer arms control processes in which civil society has become integrated—such as those on anti-personnel landmines, small arms and explosive remnants of war—also tend to put a stronger emphasis on the humanitarian dimension of the issue, and try to balance this against the military and state security concerns of many of the countries involved. Older approaches—such as the Nuclear Non-Proliferation Treaty or the Biological and Toxin Weapons Convention—only permit very limited roles for non-governmental input, and tend to avoid or underplay discussion of the humanitarian catastrophe that could be caused by the weapons systems with which they are dealing.

One reason for this difference, of course, is that the humanitarian consequences of landmines, small arms and explosive remnants of war are immediately apparent. The humanitarian consequences of nuclear or biological weapons, on the other hand—while clear to anyone who takes the time to think about it—do not appear daily on our television screens. Another important reason for this difference, however, is that civil society organizations tend to put the strongest emphasis on the humanitarian imperative, and where these organizations are not present in negotiating contexts, the humanitarian imperative tends to become overwhelmed by concerns about state and military security.

It is important, therefore, to continue to emphasize the humanitarian dimension of all aspects of disarmament and arms control. Organizations such as UNIDIR[14] and the International Committee of the Red Cross (ICRC),[15] among others, are making important contributions to this effort but more needs to be done. In particular, opening up more traditional disarmament and arms control processes to the humanitarian concerns of non-governmental bodies would be a step forward.

INFREQUENCY OF INTERACTION

Apart from the Conference on Disarmament—which is in session for more than 20 weeks each year (but which is currently deadlocked)—multilateral disarmament diplomacy on issues such as nuclear or biological weapons, for example, is characterized by brief bouts of intensive negotiation separated by long periods during which the multilateral process does not advance. This has a number of drawbacks. It means that the multilateral disarmament process proceeds in fits and starts—if it proceeds at all—and that negotiators have little opportunity in the long periods between formal negotiations to advance the process, even informally. It also means that negotiators have less opportunity to understand each other's negotiating positions, making it more difficult for them to find compromises and reach agreement.

This is not an argument for further increasing the workload of disarmament negotiators or asking them to engage in more negotiations than they already do. The multilateral disarmament calendar is already full to bursting and most diplomats in the Geneva context—especially those from smaller and developing countries—are also expected to cover a range of other issues outside the remit of disarmament and arms control. In many cases, asking them to do more work than they already do is simply not realistic. However it should be possible to provide disarmament diplomats with an informal yet structured multilateral space that they can use in the periods between formal negotiations in order to understand better one another's positions, to advance discussions and to test potential compromises. The work carried out by the Geneva Forum to support a range of disarmament and arms control processes is a good example of this approach.[16]

THE STIFLING INFLUENCE OF "PRECEDENT"

In multilateral diplomacy, the concept of precedent—relying on past practice to shape the structures for solving current problems—was designed to create stable operating procedures that would facilitate the negotiating process, allowing for steady progress to be made without the risk of negotiations coming off the rails because of some rash, untested innovation.

In the area of disarmament and arms control, precedent is especially important since states tend to be risk averse when it comes to their national security and, therefore, are wary of negotiation procedures that are radically different from those that have been employed in the past. The concept of precedent, therefore, is as indispensable a component of the disarmament and arms control machinery as it is of all legal systems.

However, the concept of precedent comprises both a conservative and a creative element. Like a ratchet, it has two functions; to allow forward movement (innovation) while preventing backsliding. Unfortunately, much of today's disarmament diplomacy overemphasizes the conservative element while underutilizing the creative element of precedent. As a result, the concept of precedent tends to constrain more than it enables multilateral disarmament negotiations and, on the whole, actually serves to stifle innovation. Although, thankfully, there are some notable exceptions, many disarmament diplomats have become too used to the idea that, "if it hasn't been done before, then we can't do it".

INADEQUATE PUBLIC AWARENESS

The International Campaign to Ban Landmines (ICBL) demonstrated the extent of the influence that can be brought to bear on multilateral disarmament processes by global public opinion. NGO coalitions that have more recently sprung up around the proliferation and misuse of small arms and light weapons, biological weapons and the use of cluster munitions are attempting to emulate the ICBL example of global awareness-raising in order to influence multilateral negotiating processes on these issues.

More generally, however, there has been a marked failure to sensitize global public opinion to the importance of some of the issues being dealt with in ongoing disarmament and arms control processes. There are of course other issues competing for the attention of the public. But when one considers some of the disarmament issues being dealt with today—the potential misuse of the ongoing revolution in biology and the lax storage conditions of significant amounts of fissile material, to take just two examples—then it is clear that new initiatives need to be undertaken to mobilize public interest.

There can be little doubt that a certain lack of transparency and weak civil society participation in some important areas of multilateral disarmament, especially concerning weapons of mass destruction, contribute to public apathy on these issues. Whatever the full range of reasons may be, however, the result of this overall failure to sensitize global public opinion has been that disarmament and arms control negotiations have tended to take place in a vacuum, immune from the productivity-enhancing influence that watching eyes can exert.

INABILITY TO "GENERATE" POLITICAL WILL

All of the above constraints make it more difficult for the existing disarmament machinery to implement effectively the will of the international community where such a will exists. They also impede the generation of political will necessary to make progress on numerous difficult issues of disarmament and arms control.

CURRENT DISARMAMENT AND ARMS CONTROL PROCESSES

All of these constraints are visible to differing degrees in different areas of multilateral disarmament and arms control. The Conference on Disarmament is an example of a "traditional" disarmament mechanism with its origins in the Cold War era. Although the Conference (along with its predecessor institutions) has an impressive list of achievements to its name—including the Nuclear Non-Proliferation Treaty, the Chemical and Biological Weapons Conventions and the Comprehensive Nuclear-Test-Ban Treaty—it has been deadlocked since 1996, unable to agree a programme of future work, except for a brief period at the end of 1998.

NGOs are excluded from the work of the CD, except for one presentation each year on International Women's Day by the Women's International League for Peace and Freedom, and the possibility for NGOs to observe plenary sessions. It is a promising sign, however, that the Conference decided in 2004 that, once it was able to get back to work on substantive issues, civil society would have more access to its deliberations.[17] While this access will still be minimal compared with other disarmament processes, it does represent progress nonetheless. And it augurs well for a possible further opening up of the work of the CD in the future.

The negotiating processes surrounding the Nuclear Non-Proliferation Treaty and the Biological and Toxin Weapons Convention, while being more open than the CD, are also somewhat insulated from civil society influences and thus are cast more in the mould of traditional disarmament processes. With the Convention on Certain Conventional Weapons and the United Nations Programme of Action on the Illicit Trade in Small Arms and Light Weapons, however, a move towards a newer approach to arms control is detectable, in which NGOs and international organizations are considered more as useful partners rather than sometimes problematic outsiders.

Finally, there is the Antipersonnel Mine Ban Convention, which is to arms control what the Guggenheim Museum in Bilbao is to architecture—an approach that transcends the constraints of traditional disarmament to create something new and never seen before. Moreover, like the Guggenheim in Bilbao, the Convention is an innovation that many people find very disconcerting to look at.

CONCLUSION

Derrida's insight into the difficulty of expressing the human will, owing to the constraints imposed on us by the means we have of expressing it, has relevance for disarmament and arms control. The structures, procedures and institutions that the international community uses to address common security challenges matter not only in determining whether or not multilateral agreements are reached, but also in determining the effectiveness of these agreements.

This paper has argued that the disarmament machinery does not just have to be a passive instrument that relies on the existence of political will to move forward. If optimized to overcome the constraints outlined above, this machinery could conceivably also contribute in a meaningful way to generating at least some of the political will necessary for addressing common security challenges.

Overall, the way in which threats to international peace and security are being defined is changing in a way that puts the humanitarian imperative closer to the centre of disarmament and arms control, where it belongs. This is largely a result of the ever more prominent role being played by civil society. The existing disarmament and arms control machinery has demonstrated on a number of occasions that it is capable of adapting to and profiting from this change. Adaptation to date has, however, been rather slow and uneven. A good deal more needs to change in order for the international community to have at its disposal effective tools to identify and respond to the collective security threats of today and tomorrow.

Notes

1   Patrick McCarthy coordinates the Geneva Forum, a joint initiative of the Quaker United Nations Office (QUNO), UNIDIR, and the Programme for Strategic and International Security Studies (PSIS) of the Graduate Institute of International Studies in Geneva. The Forum works in support of a range of disarmament and arms control processes taking place in Geneva. This is a personal contribution and does not necessarily reflect the views of the Geneva Forum partner organizations.

2   This paper is based on a presentation to a UNIDIR seminar entitled "Some Alternative Approaches in Multilateral Decision-making: Disarmament as Humanitarian Action" that took place on 3 November 2004 at the Palais des Nations in Geneva. The author is grateful to participants in this seminar for having provided useful insights and criticisms on the ideas presented, and to John Borrie and Vanessa Martin Randin for providing detailed comments on a first draft of this paper. Any remaining errors or inconsistencies are the responsibility of the author.

3   Jacques Derrida wrote over a hundred books in his lifetime. For good insights into his thinking and his conceptualization of deconstruction, the following books by Derrida are recommended: J. Derrida, *Of Grammatology*, Baltimore: Johns Hopkins University Press, 1974; *Writing and Difference*, Chigago: University of Chicago Press, 1978; *The Post Card: From Socrates to Freud and Beyond*, Chigago: University of Chicago Press, 1987. For an overview of his idea of deconstruction, see also J. D. Caputo, *Deconstruction in a Nutshell: A Conversation with Jacques Derrida*, New York: Fordham University Press, 1996.

4   By "political will", I mean the willingness of states to deal with a given problem in cooperation with other states and international actors. For an issue to be ripe for multilateral attention, a "critical mass of political

will" has first to be built up. For more on the concept of political will in connection with nuclear disarmament, see the "Reaching Critical Will" project website www.reachingcriticalwill.org.

5   Legal commentaries on negotiating processes offer detailed insights into the role played by individual diplomats on the negotiating floor. See, for example, B. Simma (ed.), *The Charter of the United Nations: A Commentary*, Oxford: Oxford University Press, 2002; and S. Maslen, *Commentaries on Arms Control Treaties Volume I—The Convention on the Prohibition of the Use, Stockpiling, Production and Transfer of Anti-Personnel Mines and on their Destruction*, Oxford: Oxford University Press, 2004.

6   The Conference on Disarmament is the successor to the Ten-Nation Committee on Disarmament (1959-1960), the Eighteen-Nation Committee on Disarmament (1962-1969), the Conference of the Committee on Disarmament (1969-1978), and the Committee on Disarmament (1979-83). For an excellent overview of the history and achievements of the CD, see J. Goldblat, *Arms Control: The New Guide to Negotiations and Agreements*, 2nd edition), London: Sage Publications, 2002, pp. 14-17.

7   The dates given are when these instruments were opened for signature.

8   The author is indebted to Professor Neil Cooper of the University of Plymouth, United Kingdom, for sharing with him an as yet unpublished paper entitled "Arms Control, Disarmament and Asymmetrical Arms Limitation", from which a number of ideas in this section are drawn.

9   T. Hobbes, *Leviathan*, Oxford: Oxford University Press, 1996.

10 *The Responsibility to Protect, Report of the International Commission on Intervention and State Sovereignty*, International Development Research Centre, Canada, 2001.

11 United Nations, *A More Secure World: Our Shared Responsibility*, 2004. See, in particular, Part I(II)C on "Sovereignty and Responsibility".

12 The NGO Global Witness produced a seminal report on conflict diamonds in 1998—*A Rough Trade: The Role of Diamond Companies and Governments in the Angolan Conflict*. As a response to this and other civil society activity on the issue, the first meeting of Southern African diamond-producing states took place in Kimberly, South Africa, in 2000. In 2002, the Kimberly Process Certification Scheme was agreed. This is a joint government, international diamond industry and civil society initiative to stem the flow of conflict diamonds.

13 United Nations General Assembly Resolution A/RES/50/70(B).
14 See, for example, *Disarmament as Humanitarian Action*, Geneva: UNIDIR, 2001. On the occasion of its twentieth anniversary, UNIDIR published this short pamphlet to refocus attention on the importance of viewing all efforts at disarmament—be they in the areas of conventional weapons or weapons of mass destruction—as essentially being humanitarian in nature. In her foreword, UNIDIR Director, Patricia Lewis, points out that "one explanation put forward [for the lack of progress in disarmament] is that governments and civil society have lost sight of the disastrous humanitarian impact of the use of weapons".
15 See, for example, *Biotechnology, Weapons and Humanity*, Geneva: ICRC, 2003 (www.scienceforhumanity.org). This ICRC initiative seeks to overcome the current inability of the Biological and Toxin Weapons Convention regime to keep pace with the revolution in the life sciences by appealing to governments and scientists to recognize and take action to prevent the potentially disastrous humanitarian consequences of the misuse of modern biotechnology.
16 For example, the Geneva Forum initiative entitled "The Geneva Process on Small Arms" contributes to the implementation of the 2001 United Nations *Programme of Action to Prevent, Combat and Eradicate the Illicit Trade in Small Arms and Light Weapons in All Its Aspects* by engaging states, international organizations and NGOs in regular consultations to share information on how they are implementing the agreement and to identify cooperative implementation arrangements. See www.geneva-forum.org.
17 CD/WP.535 (24 August 2004), p. 6. This decision was taken by the CD during its 946th plenary meeting on 12 February 2004. It allows NGOs to (a) continue to observe formal plenary meetings of the CD, (b) receive official documents of plenary meetings upon request, (c) make written material available outside the CD chamber twice per year, and (d) address one informal plenary meeting per year once the CD has succeeded in adopting a programme of work.

CHAPTER 4

A COMPARISON BETWEEN ARMS CONTROL AND OTHER MULTILATERAL NEGOTIATION PROCESSES

Vanessa Martin Randin and John Borrie

INTRODUCTION

Success in multilateral disarmament and arms control has been elusive in recent years.[1] The Geneva-based Conference on Disarmament (CD)—traditionally described as the "sole multilateral forum" for the negotiation of disarmament treaties—has been deadlocked since 1999.[2] The Ad Hoc Group process to develop a regime to the Bacteriological (Biological) and Toxin Weapons Convention (BTWC), intended to improve confidence in compliance, collapsed in early 2001 as it neared completion.[3] Crisis in the context of the BTWC five-yearly review process ensued. The protocol negotiations were succeeded from the end of 2002 by a "new process" with a deliberative mandate—a step backwards in norm-building terms from a negotiation on legally binding measures. Of Geneva-based disarmament and arms control processes only the Convention on Certain Conventional Weapons (CCW)[4] has achieved a new legally binding instrument recently with the conclusion of the Protocol V on Explosive Remnants of War (ERW) in November 2003. As of writing, however, this legally binding instrument has not yet achieved the requisite 20 ratifications to enter into force internationally. Negotiations on other priority issues in the CCW context, such as alleviating the humanitarian impact of mines other than anti-personnel mines, remain elusive.

There is growing concern that the multilateral disarmament endeavour in general may be faltering. Perhaps part of this is perceptual, in the wake of early negotiating successes such as the Chemical Weapons Convention (CWC), the Comprehensive Nuclear-Test-Ban Treaty (CTBT) and Antipersonnel Mine Ban Convention following the end of the Cold War.[5] These seemed to promise further multilateral successes to come.

Certainly, the disarmament and arms control record prior to 1989 was anything but striking. A study published that year entitled *Success and Failure in Arms Control Negotiations* observed that "despite many complex and lengthy negotiations, and despite a number of specific agreements, the result of these efforts to curb arms has been decidedly meagre to date"— referring not only to multilateral efforts and comprehensive nuclear-test-ban discussions but to Soviet-United States nuclear arms control processes and the Mutual and Balanced Force Reductions (MBFR) Talks in Europe.[6] It foretold not a hint of the rapid transformation of multilateralism's fortunes in the post-bipolar world that would shortly follow.

Fifteen years later the multilateral disarmament endeavour appears, at first glance, largely to have stalled. There is also concern over new features of the contemporary environment including retreat from certain existing norms such as the United States' withdrawal from the Anti-Ballistic Missile (ABM) Treaty in 2001 and North Korean statements of withdrawal from the Nuclear Non-Proliferation Treaty (NPT). Signs that multilateral arrangements are perceived as a troublesome burden more often than they are regarded as routes to enhanced collective security in certain governments, have accompanied it. In December 2001, for example, the United States Under-Secretary of State for Arms Control, John Bolton, explained his country's reasons for rejecting a draft compliance protocol to the BTWC in uncompromising terms: "We will continue to reject flawed texts like the BWC draft Protocol recommended to us simply because they are the product of lengthy negotiations or arbitrary deadlines, if such texts are not in the best interests of the United States and many other countries represented here today."[7]

One of the assumptions implicit in such a statement is that, like cordon bleu cuisine in a fine restaurant, negotiating products are uncovered before expectant dining governments after lengthy preparation behind closed kitchen doors. In reality, of course, the diners in this metaphor are intimately involved in the preparation and cooking of those products. Indeed, they help to write the recipes and choose the ingredients. In other words, by rejecting the BTWC draft protocol, the United States was also rejecting a product of its own making.

This suggests that difficulties experienced in disarmament and arms control negotiations are rather more complex than sometimes portrayed. Though governments may differ in their final judgements about the quality of an outcome, they each bear a share of the responsibility for their unsuccessful experiments as well as for their triumphs. If, as Mr Bolton implied, the final proof of the pudding is in the eating then it follows that attention should be paid to improving what goes on in the kitchen to make sure it is of a high standard, rather than simply on whether the diner accepts or rejects it. A better preparation and cooking process might ensure that a negotiation outcome meets with more satisfaction next time.

From the perspective of the UNIDIR Disarmament as Humanitarian Action project it begs the question: to what extent do the working practices, rules and techniques applied in multilateral disarmament and arms control negotiations contribute to (or alleviate) difficulties in achieving successful outcomes?

Looking for answers requires looking deeper for patterns than relying on explanations couched in terms of "political will", which is a term beloved by diplomats to describe the dynamics that infuse each international negotiating process. Political will is problematic because it does little to explain actual reasons for negotiating momentum or resistance. Nor does it facilitate comparison between negotiating processes. Moreover, it is not clear that political will—usually deployed as a concept external to a negotiation at the working level to describe pressure (or lack of it) from capitals, domestic constituencies, international public opinion, specific governmental friends and allies—is actually wholly distinct. Political will is instead better thought of as a shorthand term that should not be confused with substantive explanation because lack of it fails to answer questions about *why* a negotiation succeeds or fails satisfactorily. It merely indicates deeper, more specific explanations to be uncovered.[8]

Six examples of multilateral negotiating processes are examined below in order to identify factors that help—or hinder—the successful achievement of multilateral negotiating outcomes: three in the disarmament and arms control domain and three outside it.

In the next section the United Nations International Convention on the Protection of the Rights of All Migrant Workers and Members of their Families, the Framework Convention on Climate Change (FCCC) and the World Health Organization (WHO) Framework Convention on Tobacco Control (FCTC) are compared. These three processes were chosen because, although highly politically sensitive and differing in nature, they were, nevertheless, successful. In short, the authors felt it more important to learn from examples of success rather than failure. Furthermore, it was appreciated that official texts and secondary sources from these negotiations alone would not provide the insights necessary for a proper understanding of them for the purposes of comparative analysis. Our three choices reflect access to key participants in these processes, who were able to provide first-hand views that supplemented and extended our understanding of the negotiating dynamics involved.

Three Geneva-based arms control processes are then examined—the Conference on Disarmament, the protocol negotiations to the BTWC and the negotiations on the ERW Protocol to the Convention on Certain Conventional Weapons.

Chronologically this study is concerned primarily with the active negotiating phase of each of these six negotiations, although we set out aspects of the pre-negotiation of each process to provide context. In general, a basic distinction is observed between multilateral *pre-negotiation* (relating to issue definition, by whatever means), *negotiation* (relating to the drafting of commonly-agreed text) and *post-negotiation* (including signature, ratification, accession and implementation of the agreement).

Of particular interest are the individual dynamics of each negotiation: what these were, why they came about and how they can be compared. The substance of each of the six examples differs. Climate change negotiations do not share much in common in terms of subject matter with ERW, for instance. But they take place within broadly comparable, even similar, multilateral contexts and episodes in time. This paper examines whether negotiators in the disarmament and arms control field (and probably more broadly in the diplomatic community) share a *community of practice*. Such a community entails "a group of people who over a period of time share in some set of social practices geared toward some common social purpose".[9]

Although each negotiation process has its own unique properties, multilateral negotiating dynamics appear to be inherently iterative. That is, they represent fairly complex feedback mechanisms evolving dynamically on a continual basis at the human behavioural level. This "human factor" stems not only from actions of leaders or opinion shapers in each negotiation. It also stems from the ways and extent to which their views are accepted by the other negotiators within that domain.

It appears likely that these mechanisms are recursive across different negotiations, especially in hothouse multilateral environments like Geneva and New York. Multilateral negotiations stripped down to their bare bones are, after all, concerned with finding common agreement among a set of diverse participants, each with differing concerns and aims. There appear to be similarities in structure, procedure and lexicography, as we shall see. And each phase in such processes, however defined, presents challenges that may be characterized or grouped in common ways. This is not least because individual negotiators tend to accumulate their experience over time in a finite set of different multilateral areas. And negotiation structures and rules of procedure tend to be largely inherited, especially within the United Nations domain. Such diplomatic precedent is a double-edged sword.

Let us now turn to examining the negotiation of the United Nations Migrant Workers' Convention, the FCCC and the WHO FCTC.

MULTILATERAL NEGOTIATIONS IN THE FIELD OF MIGRATION, CLIMATE CHANGE AND PUBLIC HEALTH

CASE STUDIES

Migration: The United Nations International Convention on the Protection of the Rights of All Migrant Workers and Members of their Families[10]

Aim

The United Nations Convention on the Rights of Migrant Workers and Their Families is a legally binding document providing for the protection of migrant workers and their family members in the areas of civil, political, legal, economic, social and cultural rights.[11]

The process

The 1990 United Nations Migrant Workers Convention was not the first legal instrument pertaining to the rights of migrant workers. Previously the International Labour Organization (ILO) had concluded the Contracts of Employment (Indigenous Workers) Convention (No. 86) in 1947 and the *Migration for Employment Convention* (No. 97) in 1949. Moreover, in 1975 the ILO completed negotiations on a Convention concerning Migrants in Abusive Conditions and the Promotion of Equality of Opportunity and Treatment of Migrant Workers (No. 143). But this agreement, like the others that preceded it, did not receive wide international support. This was because these conventions were primarily concerned with the economic rights of migrant workers in keeping with the ILO mandate.[12] As a result, they failed to address other important rights such as social, religious and linguistic rights, which limited their appeal.

Shortly after the adoption of the 1975 ILO Convention a report was submitted to the Economic and Social Council (ECOSOC) of the United Nations on the Exploitation of Labour Through Illicit and Clandestine Trafficking.[13] The report drew attention to the "precarious positions of migrant workers around the world" and so marked the beginnings of the United Nations Convention on Migrant Workers and Their Families.[14]

The process leading to this Convention formally commenced on 17 December 1979 when United Nations General Assembly resolution 43/172 was agreed. The resolution created an open-ended working group to elaborate a treaty on the rights of migrant workers and their families. Given that the working group was open-ended, it was decided that all of its decisions would be made by consensus. This practice meant that larger groups like the Group of 77 developing states would not dominate majority decision-making by means of their superior numbers, as compared with developed nations.[15] Ambassador Gonzales de Leon of Mexico was elected Chairman of the Working Group.

The Working Group mainly comprised delegates of three kinds. First, there were experts on migration sent from capitals. Secondly, there were delegates from capitals or from the United Nations permanent delegations sent as experts on international law in the field of human rights. Lastly, there were representatives from the permanent delegations versed in United Nations politics and broader diplomacy.[16]

Ambassador de Leon was tasked with the development of the Convention text. In May 1981 he presented his first draft to the Working Group. However many Western European governments in particular were under the impression that the text condoned continued illegal immigration.

Consequently, Ambassador de Leon's text did not garner support from states that were experiencing net inflows of illegal migration. It was at this juncture that a coalition of experts from four Mediterranean and three Scandinavian states joined forces.[17] The MESCA group, as it came to be known, effectively assumed responsibility for the drafting of the Convention after 1981. Negotiations on the text continued until 18 December 1990, when work on the Convention was completed and the text adopted by the United Nations General Assembly.[18]

Difficulties in the process

The Migrant Workers Convention took almost 11 years to complete. During this period changes in global political and economic dynamics transformed patterns of worldwide movement of migrant workers. For instance, at the beginning of the process, the distinction between states that "sent" migrant workers and those that "received" them was well delineated. In the former category were mainly developing states and in the latter were industrialized states. However, over time the changing self-perceptions of some states increasingly blurred these distinctions. Changing attitudes towards migrant workers in individual countries due to changes in demographics also influenced delegates' behaviour in the negotiations. It was common for the negotiating positions of some states to shift over the duration of the drafting process. This made the process of consensus-building harder.[19]

The sheer length of the negotiations also introduced problems of a more practical nature. The Working Group saw a high turnover of delegates over the span of more than a decade. New delegates in the Working Group had to be frequently "educated" on the issues under discussion. This ultimately represented time taken away from substantive negotiations. Under these circumstances, maintaining focus on common objectives and goals for the Convention was challenging for states in the process.

Factors underpinning success

As outlined above, MESCA played an integral role in furthering momentum in negotiations after the first reading of the draft Convention in 1981. MESCA was comprised of experts from the seven states whose governments had a "decidedly socialist flavouring" in the early and middle years of the 1980s.[20] MESCA members were especially influential in laying down the structures of the draft, which thereafter formed the basis for future negotiations. This structure was based on the principle that the agreement should "discourage employers from seeking and hiring workers who are undocumented or in an irregular situation",[21] while recognizing that certain fundamental rights must be accorded irrespective of whether migrants were in a lawful or unlawful status.[22] Overall, MESCA proved beneficial in terms of providing momentum to the process and in shaping the final Convention text.

The negotiation's general parameters appear to have been another significant factor in the successful (albeit belated) completion of the Convention. Had the negotiations taken place in the ILO context, as migration issues at the multilateral level had previously, the Convention would probably have been confined to considering the economic rights of workers, rather than the broader scope to which it extended under a United Nations mandate. It appears that placed in a fresh context (the United Nations), a process that had increasingly failed to satisfy expectations in one forum (the ILO), had a positive effect on the ability of participating states to frame the issues. However the ILO was not left out in the cold entirely as the MESCA group approached the specialized agency at a later stage of the drafting process for their technical advisory services. In approaching the ILO in this manner negotiations profited from the experience and know-how of this specialized agency.

Climate change: United Nations Framework Convention on Climate Change and the Kyoto Protocol[23]

Aim
Negotiations on a legally binding framework convention relating to climate change were aimed at helping to stabilize levels of carbon dioxide and other greenhouse gas (GHG) concentrations in the atmosphere, in order to minimize the risk of dangerous human-induced interference with the climate system.[24]

The process
Scientists began to devote more attention to the possibility of climate change from the mid-1980s as evidence for its existence due to human activities accumulated. These issues moved into the political limelight in 1988 at the Toronto Conference on the Changing Atmosphere: Implications for Global Security. Following on from this, the government of Malta introduced a resolution in the United Nations General Assembly in December 1988 formally requesting the United Nations Environment

Programme (UNEP) and the World Meteorological Organization (WMO) to take steps towards the creation of a global convention on climate change. An Intergovernmental Panel on Climate Change (IPCC) was set up later that year, organized by UNEP and WMO. The three working groups of IPCC dealt with scientific and technical assessment of atmospheric changes; the social and economic impact of climate change and possible response strategies to the climate change problem.

The IPCC preliminary report, though controversial, was tabled at the Second World Climate Conference in Geneva in 1990. By that meeting's conclusion conference participants were able to agree that negotiations on FCCC should begin and that all negotiations should take place under United Nations auspices. This resulted in the United Nations General Assembly establishing the Intergovernmental Negotiating Committee (INC) for the purposes of fashioning the Framework Convention, as well as any related legal instruments it deemed necessary. The upcoming United Nations Conference on Environment and Development in Rio de Janeiro in June 1992 provided the target deadline for signature.

The INC held five sessions from February 1991: one near Washington, DC (in Chantilly, Virginia), two in Geneva with INC 3 in Nairobi in between, and the final negotiating session in New York from February to May 1992.[25] Decision 1/1 of the INC Plenary prohibited holding more than two meetings at any one time during a session or any intersessional meetings.[26] This promoted transparency in the proceedings because smaller delegations were not split between meetings in different chambers.

At the first session of the INC a bureau was elected and Jean Ripert of France appointed as Chairman.[27] According to the INC rules of procedure all substantive decisions were to be taken by consensus, although voting would be permitted when all efforts at consensus had been exhausted. The INC established two working groups: Working Group 1 dealing with the substantive issues of the FCCC; and Working Group 2 concerned mainly with procedural issues.

However, by February 1992 at INC 5 in New York there was still no resolution of some issues—particularly GHG reduction targets. The INC therefore decided to continue its work in April that year. Between the two INC 5 sessions Ripert convened an "extended bureau" meeting in Paris.[28]

At this meeting he was urged to develop his own "composite text" in order to simplify the heavily bracketed negotiating text that had developed.

A composite text under Ripert's name duly appeared before INC 5 when it resumed in April 1992. Many participants believed that this move was critical to the success of the negotiations.[29] At INC 5 it was decided to abandon the established working group structure and work instead in three groups in order to consider clusters of articles. These three groups were as follows:

- Commitments (Article 4), financial mechanisms (Article 11) and reporting chaired by Jean Ripert;
- Preamble, objectives and principles (Articles 2 and 3) chaired by Dr Ahmed Djoghlaf of Algeria;
- Institutions, dispute settlement and final clauses chaired by Ambassador Raoul Estrada of Argentina. Towards the end of the meeting this group also served as a legal drafting group and considered articles from the other clusters.[30]

After all interested delegations had been offered the opportunity to have their say on the outstanding issues, Ripert reconvened the Extended Bureau and compromises were worked out. Thanks to this deal-making, negotiations on the Framework Convention achieved completion in time for adoption at the Rio Conference on Environment and Development in 1992. Moreover, a Conference of the Parties (COP) was created, in accordance with Article 7 of the FCCC.[31] The COP meets annually and is supported by a secretariat established under Article 8 of the FCCC. Moreover, the Convention established a series of institutions to govern, manage and support continuing negotiations on protocols within its framework.[32]

The first COP to the FCCC met in Berlin in March 1995. At this meeting it was decided that negotiations should begin on a protocol or other legal instruments that would strengthen commitments under the Convention and address emission reduction beyond the year 2000.[33] This Protocol was duly negotiated and adopted by the third COP in Kyoto, Japan, in December 1997 and is known as the Kyoto Protocol.[34]

Difficulties in the negotiation of the Framework Convention

The FCCC negotiating process had to reconcile a myriad of negotiating positions among participating states. Developing countries were divided into three main groups. The first group, of small island states and some African nations, wanted the developed world to bear the brunt of responsibility for the climate change problem. The second group, including Brazil, China and India, pushed for financial and technical assistance to reduce their GHG emissions. The third group, made up of Saudi Arabia and other fossil fuel exporting countries, was concerned about the economic aspects of cutting GHGs because of potential implications for its economies. Among the developed nations the United Kingdom, for instance, was opposed to using certain fiscal measures such as carbon taxes to reduce GHG emissions while France (and, similarly, Japan) espoused carbon cuts on the basis of per capita calculations. Austria and Switzerland advocated strong commitments to reducing carbon dioxide, a position the United States did not support.[35]

Factors underpinning success

The INC Chairman played an integral role in the successful completion of the FCCC process. Ripert skilfully aided the building of consensus, most visibly through presentation of his compromise text at the end of INC 5, a contribution that has been widely acknowledged.[36] Moreover, his chairmanship appeared to provide an important sense of continuity to the negotiating process. This was especially significant because the "formal rotation of the co-chairs between working group sessions tended to limit the continuity and to obstruct the global vision needed for the success of these complex negotiations".[37]

Ripert also allowed non-governmental organizations (NGOs) access to the plenary meetings.[38] The ability of NGOs to monitor and influence the FCCC negotiating process was "enhanced by cooperation within the Climate Action Network (CAN), a network organized and run by regional groups of NGOs".[39] These NGOs worked effectively with governments and were also important in voicing the concerns of smaller island states that would be more prone to the effects of climate change. A powerful weapon in the CAN coalition's arsenal was a widely circulated newsletter it produced entitled ECO.[40] This publication helped CAN to coordinate information exchange on climate change at the national, regional and international levels. It also drew further attention to policy options and position papers on issues related to climate change and coordinated activities that the CAN NGO members produced.[41]

Consensus-building among the negotiating states may also have been helped by the high frequency of informal meetings and workshops held during and between the five INC sessions. The time line provided for by the Rio Conference, coupled with the frequency of these informal meetings and information sessions, created momentum for progress through to a successful conclusion.

Public health: the Framework Convention on Tobacco Control[42]

Aim

The objective of the WHO FCTC and its future protocols is to protect present and future generations from the health, social, environmental and economic consequences of tobacco consumption and exposure to tobacco smoke. The framework for tobacco control measures is to be implemented by states parties at the national, regional and international levels in order to reduce progressively and substantially the prevalence of tobacco use and exposure to tobacco smoke. The treaty has provisions for issues such as tobacco advertising and promotion, agricultural diversification, smuggling, taxes, and subsidies.

The process

The governing body of the WHO is the World Health Assembly (WHA). On 24 May 1999 the WHA backed a resolution (WHA 52.18) calling for work to begin on a framework convention on tobacco control. The resolution contained a detailed negotiating timetable.[43] A record 50 countries including China, France, the Russian Federation, the United Kingdom and the United States pledged their financial and political support for the prospective convention. Support was also forthcoming from countries with "major tobacco growers and exporters, as well as several developing and developed countries that face the brunt of the tobacco industry's marketing and promotion".[44]

The WHA resolution contained an annex detailing the two-stage process that would govern the development of the WHO FCTC. The first stage involved a working group open to all WHO member states. In the second stage an Intergovernmental Negotiating Body (INB) would be responsible for the drafting of the Convention and possible related protocols.

The first meeting of the Working Group took place in Geneva in October 1999; the second from 27 to 29 March 2000. The two Working Group sessions delivered a draft catalogue of possible substantive and procedural elements for the Framework Convention. A final report on the Working Group's outcome was delivered to the 53rd WHA in Geneva in May 2000. Another resolution (WHA 53.16) was unanimously adopted at that meeting: it called for negotiations to commence on the WHO FCTC. In March 2000, the WHO Director-General, Gro Harlem Brundtland, called for public hearings on issues surrounding the Framework Convention, which were held on 12 and 13 October 2000 just prior to the commencement of formal negotiations.[45]

The first of six INB sessions began in October 2000 in Geneva. The INB was open to participation by all WHO member states, regional economic integration organizations and observers. NGOs were also allowed to participate in the formal plenary sessions of the INB. The informal working group, contact group sessions and the intersessional meetings were generally closed to NGOs. However, NGOs were occasionally invited by the Chairman (with the agreement of member states) to make presentations in order to clarify issues of relevance to the discussion.[46] When the INB was in session, NGOs were also allowed time at the end of every morning and afternoon meeting to make statements. The NGO community worldwide organized themselves into the Framework Convention Alliance of which NGOs including Infact, Action on Smoking and Health (ASH) and the Campaign for Tobacco-Free Kids were prominent members.[47]

The WHO FCTC negotiations functioned largely on the basis of the six WHO regional divisions—Africa, Europe, the Eastern Mediterranean region (which encompassed the Middle East), the Western Pacific region (covering Australia, China, Japan, and most Pacific Islands), South-East Asia and the Pan-American region. The WHO sponsored regional conferences before each of the INB sessions.[48] "Regional" negotiating positions were often established at these meetings.[49]

INB 1 began its work in 2000 by reviewing the documents of the two WHO FCTC "pre-negotiation" working groups. All decisions were made by consensus and there was no voting on any matter. Three working groups were then established at the first session of the INB in Geneva and assigned with the following tasks:

- **Working Group 1**: Research; elimination of sales to and by young persons; regulation of tobacco product disclosures; packaging and labelling; demand reduction measures concerning tobacco dependence and cessation; education; training and public awareness; passive smoking and regulation of the contents of tobacco.
- **Working Group 2**: surveillance; exchange of information; price and tax measures to reduce demand for tobacco; government support for tobacco manufacturing and agriculture; illicit trade in tobacco products; licensing; guiding principles; general obligations; and definitions.
- **Working Group 3**: COP; secretariat; support by the WHO; reporting and implementation; settlement of disputes; compensation and liability; development of the convention; final clauses; financial resources; scientific; technical and legal cooperation; guiding principles; general obligations; and definitions.[50]

At INB 1 it was agreed that the Chair, Ambassador Celso Amorim of Brazil, should prepare a draft text based on member states' interventions and written submissions made at that session. Although significant progress was made on developing this text between INB 1 and INB 3, INB 4 encountered a serious hurdle. Negotiation on the text, which was by now heavily bracketed, came grinding to a halt as some delegations could not achieve compromise on provisions concerning advertising and funding.

In March 2002, during the fourth round of negotiations, it was decided that a new "Chair's text" would be developed. By now Amorim had been succeeded as INB Chair of the negotiations by Ambassador Luiz Felipe de Seixas Correa, the new Permanent Representative of Brazil in Geneva.[51] Correa's document, released in July 2002, was subsequently examined by participating states during the fifth INB session in October 2002. On the basis of these discussions Correa released a revised text on 15 January 2003 for consideration at the sixth session of the INB. In February 2003 member states agreed to transmit the final draft of the Convention to the WHA for consideration, and it was adopted on 21 May 2003.

Difficulties in the negotiation of the Framework Convention

The negotiating positions in the WHO FCTC were polarized due to the competing economic and commercial interests of various stakeholders in the process. Powerful multinational corporations including Philip Morris, Japan Tobacco and British American Tobacco (BAT) worked hard to undermine negotiations on provisions concerning tobacco advertising, promotion and sponsorship. For their part, states with large tobacco industries including Germany and the United States were initially opposed to stringent provisions on tobacco advertising, promotion and sponsorship. But some developing states and industrialized countries like Norway insisted on a tougher treaty with particular emphasis on financial aid for poorer states in implementing the pact.[52]

The system of WHO regional groups did not prove helpful in narrowing down the differences in negotiating positions among governments. While the intersessional regional meetings strengthened regional negotiating positions, the downside was that their inflexibility proved to be counter-productive at some stages of the negotiation process.

Intensive lobbying by the NGO community in the negotiations had a tendency to impede forward momentum towards completion.[53] Though well organized, NGOs were sometimes perceived, through their practice of "naming names", as lacking professionalism and political astuteness by government representatives. One example of this was a report produced by Infact entitled "Cowboy Diplomacy: How the US undermines International Environmental, Human Rights, Disarmament and Health Agreements".[54] The report was a scathing attack on the multilateral treaty record of the United States and pinpointed key individuals in the Bush Administration for their links with large tobacco corporations. Tactics such as these—however gutsy they were perceived by some—affronted the United States and other countries, making consensus-building harder.

Delegations were predominantly comprised of individuals from national ministries of health. This meant that these individuals were well versed with the subject matter under consideration. But in some cases they lacked the experience and knowledge to negotiate an international legal instrument. One delegate in the negotiations even suggested that "Many of the delegates had never heard of a 'no reservations' clause, did not know whether economic hardship constitutes a legitimate excuse under international law for non-performance of treaty obligations, and were unfamiliar with how a 'framework' convention with attached protocols is supposed to be structured".[55] Precious conference time was spent educating delegates on terminology and other legal aspects involved in multilateral negotiations.

The autonomy of some delegates participating in the negotiations also proved to be counter-productive in the long term. Delegations sometimes comprised only one or two representatives who advocated strongly for a public health agreement with detailed provisions on advertising and sponsorship. Consultation between the delegates and their ministries could be less than extensive. While this proved to be a good catalyst for progress within the negotiating process, many of these representatives subsequently encountered difficulties in obtaining domestic support for the treaty after it was completed. Arguably this has slowed down entry into force of the Convention in some countries.[56]

Factors that aided the successful conclusion of negotiations

There were a number of key factors that helped the negotiating process to a successful conclusion.

First, although they operated as individuals in the early days of the negotiations, a coalition of African, South-East Asian and Middle Eastern states, along with Caribbean and Pacific Islands, had coalesced by the last negotiating session. Together they held firm in favour of a comprehensive ban on tobacco advertising, promotion and sponsorship against powerful counteracting diplomatic pressure.[57] Moreover, this coalition was able to exact pressure on the United States and other key reluctant states to join consensus on the treaty in the last stages of the negotiations.

Secondly, there was an unprecedented amount of transparency in the proceedings. Written communications from the secretariat of the negotiation were plentiful. The secretariat regularly briefed NGOs on the substantive issues under discussion in the informal meetings, which were usually closed to NGO participation. The process also attracted much public and media attention. With the significant level of domestic public interest that the WHO FCTC process encountered, many governments came under significant pressure domestically to push for the successful conclusion of the WHO FCTC. There was also pressure from the WHO, especially Director-General Brundtland. Indeed Brundtland played an active role in the process by using her good offices to press Heads of State and heads of delegations towards completing negotiations successfully, in line with the WHO public health mandate.

Finally, when momentum in the negotiating process started to falter in INB 4 the Chairman's composite text helped to rejuvenate the process. The text that resulted from the INB 1 to INB 3 sessions (though arrived at through very transparent means) was so heavily bracketed that delegations needed guidance in reading and understanding it. The composite text produced by Chairman Correa, helped to make the text more accessible to the negotiators. This was a significant step in view of the fact that many did not have applicable legal drafting experience. Crucially the Chair achieved the authority (through his personal style and building upon the trust invested in his predecessor, Amorim) to develop a text without brackets through patient and skilled diplomacy, and brought along the vast majority of participating countries despite the contentious issues involved.

EVALUATING THE FACTORS THAT CONTRIBUTED TO SUCCESS
IN THESE MULTILATERAL NEGOTIATIONS

Each of the three multilateral negotiations discussed above was racked with political difficulties. But each appeared to benefit at least from some of the following:

- **Leadership** was important. A patient, diplomatic and knowledgeable chairperson can significantly propel negotiations as Jean Ripert aptly demonstrated in the FCCC process. A sense of timing is also a critical attribute for an effective chair especially when having to convene a "Friends of the Chair" (or in the case of the FCCC an "Extended Bureau") type of group of an executive decision-making character, as well as being a forum for private advice and views. But because they are by necessity closed (and sometimes confidential) gatherings, there paradoxically needs to be an implicit level of trust by other delegations not directly represented in the room—or at least grudging acceptance of the situation. Otherwise, solutions arrived at this way by small groups may easily unravel in the main chamber at a negotiation's conclusion. An effective leader needs to have the ability to gauge when to convene this group and whom to invite. As Seixas Correa demonstrated in the WHO FCTC process it is also important for a chairperson to understand the difficulties and needs of participants in the process and to find ways of alleviating them through judicious consultation.

On a more practical level, the chair of the negotiating body is important in providing continuity to the process. As the FCCC and the WHO FCTC process has shown it is not uncommon for the chairpersons of working groups to change from one session to another. Although this sometimes allows for more equitable state representation in the process, the chair still has to ensure that interruptions are kept to the minimum and has to have time to build sufficient credibility and knowledge to lead effectively. Another important quality for the chairperson of a negotiating body is to maintain (or least appear to maintain) a sense of autonomy from their national position. As we have seen from the United Nations Migrant Workers process, Ambassador de Leon's text did not garner support from Western states that were on the receiving end of illegal immigration. As one participant commented, "the Western European government representatives had the impression that it was basically designed to write a blank check for continued illegal migration".[58]

But leadership is not limited to the chair, as the Migrant Workers Convention process demonstrated. The MESCA group there showed that groups of individuals can transcend influence to provide collectively an element of leadership to the process.

- **Opportunities for coalition-building** among different constituents in these multilateral negotiating processes sometimes enabled weaker parties to maximize their influence and thereby better defend their interests. This was demonstrated well by the coalition of developing countries in the final stages of the WHO FCTC process. Other coalition-building efforts improved the lobbying capabilities of NGOs in processes like the FCCC. But coalition-building can also hinder consensus-building in a process—as NGO activities in the WHO FCTC process showed. This example serves to show that effective coalition-building rests not only on the sheer number or size of a coalition's members, but also on their ability to operate sensitively in a politically charged environment.

- **Informal meetings** and "non-official" contacts between negotiators were useful in the evolution of these processes. In general, informal plenary sessions abandon any structured seating plan and communication is less guarded given that these sessions are in most negotiations closed to public participation and formal records are not kept. These meetings often provided good opportunities for straight talking and clarification among negotiators, which (in principle at least) should have assisted in problem-solving. However, the WHO FCTC negotiations showed that informal meeting processes needed to be managed with care. The informal regional group meetings, between INB sessions of the WHO FCTC, hardened group positions, which compounded inflexibility back at the formal negotiating table.

- **A clear end goal, including a time frame,** appears to have been important in all three negotiations. While a quick result is not necessarily superior to a long process when complex issues need to be understood and incorporated into a realistic outcome, it may be that some degree of psychological pressure on negotiators is useful in focusing minds on facilitating agreement, as well as those of government authorities at home. The FCCC was negotiated with the Rio Conference as its deadline while the WHO FCTC process worked to a well-defined (although not immutable) timetable. In contrast the United Nations Working Group on the Convention on Migrant Workers and Their Families was not bound to any deadlines or schedules. Of course, this in itself is not sufficient: political attention and willingness to compromise in good faith at a senior level are crucial, as discussion of BTWC in the following section will show. It is probably significant that both the FCCC and the international tobacco control negotiations received considerable attention from NGOs and the wider public. By contrast, negotiation on migrant worker issues, which tended to be perceived in cross-cutting ways by differing domestic constituencies of various negotiating states, took longer.

THE CONFERENCE ON DISARMAMENT,
THE BACTERIOLOGICAL (BIOLOGICAL) AND
TOXIN WEAPONS CONVENTION AND THE CONVENTION
ON CERTAIN CONVENTIONAL WEAPONS SINCE THE 1990S

CASE STUDIES

The Conference on Disarmament

Aim

The Conference on Disarmament (CD) has a mandate to negotiate arms control and disarmament measures in any major area of interest to the international community.[59] The CD's agenda for negotiations draws from the recommendations made to it by the General Assembly, the proposals presented by member states of the Conference and the decisions of the Conference.[60]

The process

The Conference on Disarmament is a standing body and is not purely oriented towards completion of a specific negotiation unlike the processes discussed previously in this article. In accordance with Rule 18 of its rules of procedure the Conference conducts "its work and adopts its decisions by consensus".[61]

The Conference on Disarmament meets each year in Geneva in a session divided into three parts.[62] Although the CD is regarded as a body autonomous from the United Nations, the two inevitably have a close relationship in view of the CD's physical location (in the United Nations Palais des Nations), because United Nations personnel service it and because even its budget is included within the United Nations budgetary framework. In addition the Secretary-General of the CD is appointed directly by the United Nations Secretary-General in consultation with the CD and acts as his personal representative.[63] Moreover, the majority of personnel from diplomatic missions in Geneva participating in the CD also have responsibilities for servicing other disarmament or arms control-related activities there, including negotiations within United Nations frameworks.

The Presidency of the Conference on Disarmament rotates among all its members based on the English alphabetical list of membership. Each President presides over the Conference for a four-working-week period.[64] An informal "troika" system, comprising the past, present and future presidents of the Conference, exists outside the rules of procedure, intended by the Conference's membership to ensure some degree of continuity in leadership in view of the rotational process.

Members of the Conference on Disarmament operate a group system consisting of the Western European and Others Group (WEOG) of states, the Group of Eastern European States and Others, the Non-Aligned Movement as well as China. China stands outside the group system by choice, and represents itself at presidential consultations. These groups usually meet on a weekly basis when the CD is in session and appoint coordinators and special representatives occasionally on specific issues. Correspondingly, the presidential troika meets with the regional group coordinators on a weekly basis when the Conference is in session. The existence of the regional groupings assists with procedural aspects like the rotation of chairpersons in the ad hoc committees.

The Conference on Disarmament is not universal in its membership. Nor does it necessarily have the broadest active participation amongst its members in practice.[65] At present these number 66 countries, and new members may only be admitted through a consensus decision by the Conference.[66] Specialized agencies, the International Atomic Energy Agency (IAEA) and other organs of the United Nations may also be invited to participate in the work of the conference under rule 41, although the CD has never offered such an invitation. Moreover, the Conference is notable for the especially limited degree of access it affords NGOs interested in observing or contributing to its work. NGOs may attend formal plenary in the public gallery, but in effect are able to contribute little else.[67]

At the First Special Session on Disarmament in 1978 the United Nations General Assembly mandated the Conference to deal with disarmament in the following areas:

1. Nuclear weapons in all aspects;
2. Chemical weapons;
3. Other weapons of mass destruction;
4. Conventional weapons;

5. Reduction of military budgets;
6. Reduction of armed forces;
7. Disarmament and development;
8. Disarmament and international security;
9. Collateral measures, confidence building measures, and effective verification methods in relation to appropriate disarmament measures; and
10. A comprehensive programme of disarmament leading to general and complete disarmament under effective international control.[68]

As part of its rules of procedure the Conference on Disarmament adopts an agenda for each annual session in which these priorities are incorporated. At the 2004 session its agenda was as follows:

1. Cessation of the nuclear arms race and nuclear disarmament;
2. Prevention of nuclear war, including all related matters;
3. Prevention of an arms race in outer space (PAROS);
4. Effective international arrangements to assure non-nuclear-weapon states against the use or threat of use of nuclear weapons;
5. New types of weapons of mass destruction and new systems of such weapons; radiological weapons;
6. A comprehensive programme of disarmament;
7. Transparency in armaments; and
8. Consideration and adoption of the annual report and any other report, as appropriate, to the United Nations General Assembly.[69]

The crucial difficulty for the CD in undertaking substantive work, however, has been in agreeing its annual programme of work, rather than its agenda, since the conclusion of the CTBT negotiations in the mid-1990s. The programme of work comprises a schedule of the Conference's activities for the annual session taking into account the recommendations, proposals and decisions of member states of the Conference, based on the agenda.[70] A "provisional agenda and the programme of work is drawn up by the president of the Conference with the assistance of its Secretary General and presented to the Conference for consideration and adoption".[71]

The CD gathers in formal and informal plenary meetings.[72] Historically, however, most substantive work has been carried out in subsidiary bodies established by formal decision in plenary, including ad hoc committees, working groups, technical groups and groups of governmental experts.[73] Although not subsidiary bodies, "special coordinators" have also been appointed by the Presidency to look at substantive and procedural aspects of the Conference's work and have sometimes convened consultations with regional groups or the collective membership.

Rule 23 of the CD's rules of procedure states that the "Conference shall define the mandate for each of such subsidiary bodies and provide appropriate support for their work". For example, in the case of the CTBT negotiations, its mandate directed an ad hoc committee to "negotiate intensively on a universal and multilaterally and effectively verifiable comprehensive nuclear-test-ban treaty".[74] Document CD/1238 also outlined how work for this negotiation should be organized in requesting the ad hoc committee to "establish the necessary working groups" to include "one on verification and one on legal and institutional issues which should be established in the initial stage of the negotiations, and any other which the Committee may subsequently decide upon". In practice, the mandates of these committees have to be renewed annually by consensus of the Conference, with the chairing of these committees usually rotating yearly among the regional groups.

The CD annually transmits a report of its work to the United Nations General Assembly in line with its rules of procedure (rule 43). Additionally, when negotiations on legally binding instruments have been concluded in the CD (and though it is not formally obligated to do so), it has transmitted the text of these treaties to the United Nations General Assembly for endorsement along with a request for signature and ratification by United Nations Member States.

Difficulties in the process

The CD has been unable to agree on a programme of work since 1998, which means it has not undertaken substantive negotiation on any subject. The crux of the problem hinges on disagreement over the mandates to be given to subsidiary bodies to deal with PAROS and fissile material.[75] While China wanted negotiations to begin on PAROS the United States only wanted negotiations on a fissile material treaty. As consensus is needed for agreement on a programme of work, the CD became deadlocked, and remains so at the beginning of 2005.

A succession of CD Presidents—although by no means all—have tried to broker a solution in order to break this deadlock. They include efforts by Ambassadors Saleh Dembri of Algeria in 1999, as well as Jean Lint of Belgium and subsequently Celso Amorim in 2000. Although Brazil came particularly close in August 2000, Amorim's proposals could not ultimately achieve final consensus on the Conference floor.

Since then the most significant attempt to try to bring the Conference to consensus on a programme of work was a so-called "five ambassadors" (or "A5") proposal at the end of the 2002 session.[76] This proposal tabled as CD/1692 proposed the establishment of four ad hoc committees dealing with Fissile Material, Negative Security Assurances (NSA), Nuclear Disarmament and PAROS. It was also proposed that "special coordinators" on Comprehensive Disarmament, Transparency in Armaments and Radiological Weapons be appointed. However, only the Ad Hoc Committee on Fissile Material would have a negotiating mandate in accordance with the Shannon Report of 24 March 1995 (CD/1299).[77] With regard to PAROS, CD/1692 proposed that the committee should "deal with" the issue of PAROS and "identify and examine, without limitation and without prejudice, any specific topics or proposals, which could include confidence-building or transparency measures, general principles, treaty commitments and the elaboration of a regime capable of preventing an arms race in outer space". However China maintained that the language contained in the PAROS mandate was too weak. The issue boiled down ultimately to whether the word "negotiate" should or should not be included.

China belatedly submitted its own revision to the A5 proposal on 7 August 2003 stating that it was willing to accept an ad hoc committee on PAROS with "the *possibility of negotiating* a relevant international legal instrument". Many CD delegations hoped this concession would help bring an end to the impasse and that substantive work could begin. However, in a move that surprised many, the United States announced that it had decided to conduct an inter-agency process to review its policy on the negotiation of a treaty to ban the production of plutonium and highly-enriched uranium for nuclear weapons, which would delay its agreement to commence any negotiations in the CD.

United States Ambassador Jackie Sanders informed the Conference of the results of this review on 29 July 2004. Although the United States would be willing to begin negotiations on a fissile material treaty, she said, the review had concluded that effective verification of the treaty "was not achievable", promising that experts from Washington would brief the Conference on the reasons why in more detail later.[78]

Reasons for difficulties in the CD

Difficulties in finding agreement on a programme of work in the Conference on Disarmament primarily reflect the divergence in negotiating priorities that now exist among a handful of key member states, among which security threat perceptions and priorities increasingly diverge. For instance, while most delegations in the CD have expressed willingness to commence negotiations on fissile materials, other states like China believe that in the light of United States plans to build a national missile defence system, a PAROS treaty is also necessary. At root, these reflect wider geo-strategic and political calculations by these states. For instance, it has been speculated that lack of action in the Conference provides a longer window for China, which has smaller fissile material stocks for weapons than the United States or the Russian Federation, to produce and modernize its nuclear arsenal.[79] The United States, for its part, does not want to be constrained in the testing and deployment phases of its ballistic missile defence system—as demonstrated by its withdrawal from the ABM Treaty.

In other words, deadlock on substantive work in the Conference on Disarmament is not so painful for either the United States or China that they appear inclined to compromise on their opposing positions further. The structure of the Conference's procedures—particularly the consensus rule and its comparative lack of transparency—facilitates this blockage.

The Bacteriological (Biological) and Toxin Weapons Convention Protocol negotiations

Aim

The Convention bans biological weapons and the equipment and means of delivery by which such weapons can be deployed.[80] But the enforcement of the BTWC is weak and so there have followed efforts to strengthen confidence in compliance.

The process

Towards the end of the 1960s an internal review in the Nixon Administration of the United States concluded that its massive biological weapons programme should be abolished, as it was recognized that a biological arms race was not in the United States' strategic interests. Although customary international law and the 1925 Geneva Protocol banning the use of asphyxiating gases also place taboos on germ warfare, the United States, backed by other countries including the United Kingdom, felt a specific agreement banning biological weapons was necessary.[81] In 1972 negotiation of the Convention was completed, with the United States, the United Kingdom and the Soviet Union as treaty depositories. It entered into force in 1975 after 22 ratifications had been achieved. Despite its prohibitions, the Convention did not include any mechanisms to ensure confidence in compliance. Clandestine biological weapons programmes continued in some states, including in the Soviet Union, in South Africa and elsewhere.[82]

The need to strengthen the BTWC regime was acknowledged by its members at an early stage in the treaty's review process.[83] The BTWC Second Review Conference in 1986 developed a series of politically binding confidence-building measures, which were adopted and further expanded upon at the next review meeting in 1991. Also at that 1991 meeting states parties agreed to annual exchanges of selected information on facilities and activities considered relevant to BTWC compliance, including unusual outbreaks of infectious disease, vaccine production facilities, and biodefence programmes. These were effectively voluntary, however, and such reporting has always been patchy.

The 1991 Gulf war between Coalition forces (led by the United States) and Iraq as well as information leaking from the former Soviet Union about clandestine biological warfare activities there exacerbated concern in the international community that the Convention lacked means of ensuring compliance with its prohibitions. Therefore the Third Review Conference set up a group of verification experts, (known as the VEREX group) to examine potential BTWC verification measures from a scientific and technical standpoint as well as the feasibility of a compliance regime. In September 1993 VEREX issued a report concluding that certain combinations of verification measures could increase transparency, enhance confidence in compliance, and deter violations.[84] Consequently, a Special Session of BTWC in 1994 set up a further governmental group mandated to develop further the potential verification measures listed by the VEREX group and to explore the possibility of creating a legally binding instrument to strengthen the BTWC.[85]

The BTWC Ad Hoc Group negotiations were set up to achieve a legally binding protocol "as soon as possible", based on a mandate from the Fourth BTWC Review Conference in 1996.[86] According to its mandate, all Ad Hoc Group decisions were to be made by consensus. The Group negotiated from 1995 to 2001, at first on working papers submitted by national governments and later on the basis of a "rolling text" of the emerging draft protocol. Overall around three Ad Hoc Group sessions were held each year, each lasting two to three weeks. There were 24 sessions held in all, with work most intensive in 1999 and 2000 by which time the rolling text and associated documents totalled nearly 600 pages of square-bracketed or provisionally agreed language.

Difficulties in negotiating the BTWC Protocol

From the beginning of the Ad Hoc Group negotiations certain key states in the BTWC context were ambivalent about the prospect of a verification instrument. Trilateral biological weapons inspections involving the United States, the United Kingdom and the Russian Federation in the early 1990s following Russian President Yeltsin's admission that his new country had inherited the former Soviet Union's biological warfare programme had mixed consequences. In particular, the mishandling of a visit to a Pfizer biological facility in the United States had turned some of the American life science sector against compliance activities they regarded as intrusive—a description that became increasingly encompassing as the decade wore on. Investigation of Iraq's biological warfare activities by United Nations Special Commission (UNSCOM) inspectors was also encountering many difficulties.[87]

The United States' ambivalence about the value of a protocol handicapped the prospects of a robust instrument from the start. It meant that the United States failed to provide the leadership it had demonstrated elsewhere, for instance in the CWC negotiations, that could help overcome resistance from hardliners in the Non-Aligned Movement such as China, Cuba, India, Iran and Pakistan. Moreover, as the draft protocol text was fleshed out and efforts intensified towards completion by the beginning of this decade, there were growing signs of the United States officials' concerns that a compliance regime could interfere with the United States' national security activities. The United States government's reservations in public primarily hinged on the draft protocol not being sufficiently robust, and on creating risks of loss of proprietary commercial information for industry. Behind closed doors its positions on aspects of the prospective regime such as routine-type visits to check declarations, investigations and declarations contributed manifestly to the draft regime's dilution as well as undermining Western Group political unity. Moreover, hardline United States rhetoric on export controls and assistance and cooperation measures in the Ad Hoc Group exacerbated ideological polarization between developed and developing countries and was eagerly seized upon by so-called hardliners on the far end of the spectrum (many of which the United States suspected of offensive biological activities) who were no keener on a protocol than Washington appeared to be.[88]

The Russians remained largely silent in the negotiations, except on issues concerning basic definitions and "objective criteria" in which they appeared to have an interest in creating quantity thresholds for biological weapons. This would have completely undermined the object and purpose of the Convention had it been agreed because it would have undermined the treaty's basic prohibitions. The British delegation, for its part, found itself in the thankless—and increasingly impossible—position of trying to bridge the Atlantic amid growing suspicions by France, Germany and other Europeans about the posture of an increasingly exasperated United States. In sum, as the negotiations wore on, moderate countries both in the Western Group and the Non-Aligned Group who thought they had joined a process tasked with negotiating a verification regime found themselves increasingly marginalized.

Amidst all of this the Chairman of the negotiations, Ambassador Tibor Tóth of Hungary tried to edge negotiations towards completion of a final product in time for the next BTWC Review Conference in December 2001. By late 2000, however, there were ominous signs that the "endgame" process was unravelling as some delegations indicated their unwillingness to compromise on key issues in order to bring negotiations to a successful conclusion. Tóth unveiled a "composite text", based on his assessment of what the market would bear in terms of an agreement, in early 2001. In July 2001, however, the United States announced that it rejected the rolling text, the Chairman's composite text and further efforts to continue Ad Hoc Group negotiations. Ad Hoc Group collapse ensued.

Reasons for the failure of legally binding efforts to strengthen the Convention

On 25 July 2001, in a statement to the Ad Hoc Group, Ambassador Donald Mahley of the United States delegation outlined the ostensible reasons for the United States' rejection:

> The draft protocol will not improve our ability to verify BWC compliance. It will not enhance our confidence in compliance and will do little to deter those countries seeking to develop biological weapons. In our assessment, the draft Protocol would put national security and confidential business information at risk.[89]

At the Fifth Review Conference that followed in November 2001, the United States Under-Secretary of State for International Security Arms Control, John Bolton, called for the termination of the Ad Hoc Group's mandate and instead pressed for voluntary national measures to strengthen the Convention as sufficient. Bolton said it was necessary to "look beyond traditional arms control measures to deal with the complex and dangerous threats posed by biological weapons".[90]

However, while it is true that the United States was responsible for formal rejection of the draft protocol it would be a misrepresentation to claim that this explained the failure of efforts to strengthen the Convention through legally binding measures. In theory the protocol negotiations could have continued beyond July 2001 until at least the November Review Conference without the participation of the United States. And even then, had the bulk of other states parties to the Convention agreed to continue developing the protocol or other legally binding measures, procedural mechanisms existed in the rules of procedure of the Review Conference for this to have been put to a vote.[91]

None of this transpired for many reasons. One reason was because other countries with sizeable life-science sectors were reluctant to accept an inspection and declaration burden the United States (the country with the largest sector of all) would not assume. The United States' reservations and delays in implementation CWC during the late 1990s had created significant resentment, especially among European countries otherwise generally in favour of robust compliance measures. Additionally, although many countries still believed the draft protocol would be of some use in monitoring compliance if agreed, few or none held the conviction that it was very robust after years of dilution of its contents during the Ad Hoc Group's work. Political polarization in the later stages of the negotiations, as described above, also mitigated against the possibility of a strong international front materializing, especially between developed and developing countries. Perhaps most of all, however, the United States' rejection of the protocol and its negotiation process suited the so-called hardliners in the Non-Aligned Movement: failure to agree on an instrument they did not want (and may have rejected down the track) could be blamed upon the United States.

Negotiations on a protocol to the Convention on Certain Conventional Weapons on explosive remnants of war

Aim

This United Nations Convention regulates the use of certain conventional weapons in armed conflict, in order to prevent unnecessary suffering to combatants and indiscriminate harm to civilians. The CCW is a framework instrument with specific additional rules set out in subsidiary protocols.[92] Efforts since the Second CCW Review Conference have focused on minimizing the effects of explosive remnants of war (ERW), "mines other than anti-personnel mines" and enhancing compliance with the Convention, which led to agreement on a legally binding treaty on ERW in November 2003.

The process

To examine the ERW protocol negotiations, further background about the shape of the wider CCW treaty process is necessary. Negotiated in 1979 and 1980, the Convention built upon established customary rules regulating the conduct of hostilities and the provisions of the 1949 Geneva Protocol.[93] When the Convention entered into force in 1983 (three years after its adoption) it contained three protocols prohibiting the use of weapons that employ fragments undetectable in the human body by X-ray (Protocol I), regulations on the use of landmines, booby traps and similar devices (Protocol II) as well as rules limiting the use of incendiary weapons (Protocol III).

A fourth protocol was developed in 1995 that prohibits the use and transfer of blinding laser weapons.[94] At the first CCW Review Conference meeting in 1996 various changes were made to Protocol II—including expanding its scope to internal armed conflicts, as well as inter-state conflict. The Review Conference also decided that an annual meeting of state parties to Amended Protocol II would be held once sufficient ratifications had been achieved.

Momentum for a new protocol to the Convention on "explosive remnants of war" was initially generated due to efforts by the International Committee of the Red Cross (ICRC).[95] In September 2000 the ICRC organized a workshop with diplomats and military experts in Nyon, Switzerland, at which it proposed that negotiations on an ERW protocol commence at the earliest possible date within the CCW framework. This influential meeting underscored the humanitarian problems caused by ERW in recent conflicts in Kosovo, Afghanistan and Iraq (after the first Gulf war).[96]

Preparatory meetings of CCW member states were convened in December 2000 and in April 2001 to prepare for the Second Review Conference held in December 2001 and chaired by Ambassador Les Luck of Australia.[97] This was a successful meeting, including achievement of agreement to modify the scope of the CCW to encompass internal armed conflicts in addition to international conflicts.[98] The Review Conference decided to establish a "Governmental Group of Experts" to examine the possibility of a new ERW protocol. This group was to "consider all factors, appropriate measures and proposals, in particular:

- Factors and types of munitions that could cause humanitarian problems after a conflict;
- Technical improvements and other measures for relevant types of munitions, including submunitions, which could reduce the risk of such munitions becoming ERW;
- The adequacy of existing international humanitarian law in minimising post-conflict risks of ERW, both to civilians and to the military;
- Warning to the civilian population, in or close to, ERW-affected areas, clearance of ERW, the rapid provision of information to facilitate early and safe clearance of ERW, and associated issues and responsibilities; and
- Assistance and cooperation."[99]

The Group of Governmental Experts met three times in 2002. Following these discussions CCW member states decided in December of that year that the work of the Group should continue through 2003 with a mandate to negotiate. The ERW negotiation, coordinated by Geneva-based Netherlands Ambassador Chris Sanders, quickly fleshed out a draft instrument in time for agreement for adoption at the 2003 meeting of state parties the following November.[100]

The Group's discussions encompassed other issues. France (and later the European Union) put forward proposals to improve the weak compliance regime of the CCW. The ICRC concerns about the humanitarian impacts of "mines other than anti-personnel mines"—that is, anti-tank or anti-vehicle mines—in post-conflict situations were taken up in discussions. Switzerland (with ICRC support) called for further work on examining the implications of small calibre ammunition that could have so-called "dum-dum" effects. Switzerland's proposal found little resonance in the Group despite its ballistic testing that indicated some forms of military ammunition such as explosive .50 calibre bullets, apparently intended for use as anti-materiel tasks, could have dum-dum type effects in the human body (prohibited by the 1868 St. Petersburg and 1899 Hague Declarations).[101] These issues encountered different levels of acceptance amongst the majority of CCW states parties. ERW is the only item to have been negotiated upon to date.

Difficulties in the process

Earlier in the history of CCW there had been some disappointment about the outcome of negotiations on Amended Protocol II, completed in 1996, among some states and transnational civil society groups, especially in the humanitarian field. Some countries, as well as the ICRC and the International Campaign to Ban Landmines (ICBL), felt that humanitarian imperatives had been subordinated to orthodox arguments of national security and "military utility". This dissatisfaction contributed to international momentum for negotiation of the 1997 Mine Ban Convention banning antipersonnel mines, rather than merely restricting aspects of their design and use as CCW Amended Protocol II had done. A perception developed among some in the humanitarian community, as well as some core countries in the Mine Ban Convention process, that the CCW was increasingly outmoded and lacking in credibility.

Hence, there were uneven expectations about the ability of the CCW to make much progress in confronting challenges considered to be of contemporary relevance by the international community in the lead-up to the 2001 Review Conference. However, low-key but highly effective chairing by Australia created a sense at this Conference that achievement of a positive outcome would be a crucial litmus test for the CCW regime. It ultimately translated into mandates for further work in several areas.

The success of the Second CCW Review Conference formed the foundation for success in the ERW Protocol negotiation process, which nevertheless encountered difficulties in three main areas. First, there were political differences of opinion concerning its scope. Some states and NGOs felt a protocol should incorporate specific technical measures to improve the reliability of munitions (and hence lower the risk of them becoming ERW). These proposals were unable to achieve consensus in the two-year time frame of discussion and negotiation. Others felt the protocol should be only concerned with generic post-conflict remedial measures such as warnings to civilians, general undertakings to clear contaminated areas and information exchange, which seemed more broadly acceptable. Secondly, there was the issue of whether existing ERW problems would be dealt with in the instrument. Thirdly, and of particular concern to key military states such as the United States, was the principle of user-responsibility and how this might play out in terms of legal liability for users of munitions that failed to function as intended with deleterious humanitarian consequences. There was also debate over the final status of the document—that is, whether it would be legally or politically binding in nature (an option preferred by the United States). However, this was tactical rather than substantive, and hinged upon the nature of the substantive provisions on the issues outlined above.

In the end, although the majority of CCW member states held firm to their preference for a legally binding protocol, a more limited scope prevailed, which excluded firm undertakings on existing ERW (although voluntary undertakings were not excluded) and strong provisions on user-responsibility. The legal commitments agreed in CCW Protocol V are also quite qualified in many places with phrases such as "where possible" and "where feasible". So far there has been slow uptake of accessions to the Protocol: as of writing this more than a year later only a handful of countries have joined, and no states yet with major military forces such as China, the Russian Federation, the United States, the United Kingdom or France.[102]

Factors in success

In view of the paucity of positive developments in the creation of new multilateral norms in the field of disarmament and arms control in recent years the achievements of the CCW process have helped to move it from its position near the margins of the diplomatic wilderness in the 1990s closer to centre stage. There is reason to assume also that those countries unwilling to join the Mine Ban Convention, like the United States, view the CCW as a forum to show they can play a positive role on conventional weapons issues.

The preparatory process leading up to the Second Review Conference functioned as a pre-negotiation phase through its technical and diplomatic discussions and development of mandates establishing the basic parameters for work from 2001. Aiding it in this case was the modular nature of the mandate structure—a multi-lane highway rather than a one-lane road—enabling some work (amendment of the CCW to include internal armed conflict, ERW) to move faster than other traffic. However, ultimately all of this depended upon sufficient flexibility from states in the diplomatic context to avoid deadlock, as occurred in the Conference on Disarmament. The influence of key office holders at the Review Conference in this respect—Ambassador Luck of Australia and, later, Ambassador Rakesh Sood of India, in particular—was significant here in generating good will. Had a key state in the CCW had major issues with priorities or the elements of further work, this "multi-lane" system could easily have worked against the CCW making progress because of the opportunity for political linkages to be established.

An important factor in the success of the ERW protocol negotiations was the involvement of the humanitarian community including United Nations agencies, the ICRC and NGOs such as Human Rights Watch, Handicap International and Landmine Action (UK). Many of these actors were more experienced than they had been before owing to the political experience they had obtained in processes such as the Antipersonnel Mine Ban Convention. Consequently, while NGO coordination and influence never equalled that of the Mine Ban Convention process, civil society actors nevertheless interacted effectively with government representatives at the negotiations in adding both field perspectives to discussions of the effects of ERW as well as an additional sense of urgency and purpose to the negotiations. Military and diplomatic practitioners in the CCW process were also by now more accustomed to the presence of civil society actors because of the educative influence of other multilateral processes in which they had been involved like the Mine Ban Convention. The role of the Netherlands, which coordinated the ERW negotiation, was significant in this regard as a country with both military credentials (as a member of the North Atlantic Treaty Organisation (NATO) and good lines of communication with civil society.

The humanitarian influence in the ERW protocol process was especially important because it contributed to the sense among those states unhappy with aspects of the draft protocol that they should nonetheless avoid creating linkages that would prevent a successful negotiation. Negotiations took place against the backdrop of the war and opening months of Coalition occupation of Iraq, from which mounting evidence was accumulating in the media of the humanitarian consequences of ERW. Moreover, the broader CCW working structure allowed those issues unable to achieve consensus to be deferred by means of further discussion, including technical measures, specific regulations with concern to the use of cluster submunitions and discussions on the adequacy of international humanitarian law principles in this domain. This created a sense of there being a continuum of options that can avoid, or postpone, outright rejection of an issue, rather than a one-shot deal.

COMPARING DISARMAMENT AND ARMS CONTROL PROCESSES

In the next section we shall compare the six processes discussed in this article directly. However, before doing so it is worth briefly comparing and contrasting the Conference on Disarmament, BTWC and CCW Protocol V negotiation processes.

These three processes possess quite different negotiating structures. Although set up as an adjunct to a broader political process in the form of the five-yearly Review Conferences and preparatory meeting cycle, the BTWC protocol negotiations were (throughout the late 1990s until 2001 when they collapsed) the only game in town for strengthening of the norm against biological weapons. BTWC states parties were focused on one process—the Ad Hoc Group—and on one outcome. That goal was intended to be a regime designed to verify, or at least enhance confidence in, compliance with the prohibitions of the BTWC. Although broadly a *unitary* goal, the complexity of devising a comprehensive and effective regime that would be simultaneously politically acceptable proved too difficult.

By contrast, the Conference on Disarmament and the CCW process represent broader frameworks for negotiation. Such frameworks have their pluses and minuses, as shown by their contrasting experiences. In the CCW process the smorgasbord of options for substantive work, such as the post-conflict remedial effects of ERW, compliance, mines other than anti-personnel mines and the regulation of the design or use of weapons that may cause a particular humanitarian problem (like submunitions), opened up negotiating space. The process called for initial prioritization of work (post-conflict remedial measures on ERW) without foreclosing the option of revisiting other priorities later through an annual CCW meeting process established at the 2001 review meeting.

This has helped to enable negotiating actors in the CCW process to recognize the incremental nature of the process and to accept that there will be other, further opportunities to shape the achievement of their national goals. At the same time, the mandates of the Group of Governmental Experts throughout the development of the ERW negotiation process provided useful targets—both for those participants eager to achieve a positive negotiating outcome and for those with other priorities waiting in the queue, such as mines other than anti-personnel mines. Nevertheless, the ERW protocol process did not guide itself: it required deft steering and leadership to achieve completion, from the Second CCW Review Conference preparatory process onwards.

At first glance, the Conference on Disarmament—as a broad framework for negotiating on disarmament and arms control issues of importance to the international community—should possess similar advantages in terms of its annual setting of priorities and opportunities for give-and-take across its agenda and work programme. In fact, the opposite has turned out to be the case. Linkages created in the CD over differing issues (fissile negotiations and PAROS) have stymied substantive work on any of the agenda items before the Conference.

The CD and the BTWC Ad Hoc Group process share a common failing. In both cases their working structures made it difficult for their mandates to adapt to changing circumstances. The Ad Hoc Group mandate in 1996 and the CD's "decalogue" (originating from the first United Nations Special

Session on Disarmament [UNSSOD I] in 1978), with fissile material negotiations confirmed as the next negotiating step by the Shannon mandate in 1995, lost consensus support over time. The Ad Hoc Group, receiving mixed signals as it was from the United States throughout the protocol negotiation, was unable to change its trajectory before the Fifth Review Conference, especially as no clear alternative was presented in the midst of increasing political polarization in that process by the turn of the new century. The CD's difficulties have been compounded by its outmoded agenda, and inflexible procedural rules, which have so far prevented the majority of its membership from agreeing on resuming its work for fear of exacerbating differences further and inviting sabotage of their substance. At the same time, the CD's regional group structure and opaque system of consultation have prevented the development of external pressure on those members in deadlock to be more flexible in their positions. In the CD, a rotational chair every four working weeks has been an added handicap because it is an insufficient period in which a new president might reasonably be expected to build understanding and foster compromise on complex or contentious issues.

The CCW process has also enjoyed a greater degree of involvement from non-state actors such as United Nations agencies, other international organizations such as the ICRC and NGOs, than either the BTWC processes or the CD. This has not been for want of interest by transnational civil society. Rather, it is because of the traditional manner in which international security issues at the multilateral level are conceptualized by many states participating in them in terms of "state threats" and "national security". However, the input of humanitarian actors and the greater transparency brought to the CCW process by civil society appears to have benefited it in terms of generating momentum and support from domestic authorities, who were also lobbied by the ICRC, Red Cross and Red Crescent Societies and members of the NGO community. Such constituencies do not operate in the CD context, and did not exist in the BTWC protocol contexts, because they have not been nourished by governments or permitted access within the terms of their processes.

COMPARING ARMS CONTROL PROCESSES
WITH THE UNITED NATIONS MIGRANT WORKERS
CONVENTION, FCCC AND THE WHO FCTC

In the preceding sections the CD, the BTWC and the CCW protocol negotiations on ERW were outlined along with three multilateral negotiations on climate change, migration and tobacco control. What do they indicate about the extent to which working practices and rules applied in multilateral disarmament and arms control negotiations contribute to— or alleviate—difficulties in achieving successful outcomes?

At the outset it is apparent that the six processes share much in common in the types of negotiating mechanisms used and the modus operandi of their participants (not to mention some participants, such as Celso Amorim of Brazil) despite the different substantive tasks for which they were devised. Commonalities ranging from consensus decision-making, the structure of negotiating mandates and rules of procedure largely generated by means of diplomatic precedent, constitute examples of *formal* elements of a recognizable community of practice. This is reinforced by many common *informal* elements in these negotiations. But there are also some significant differences. These are as follows:

STATE PARTICIPATION

Negotiations on the ERW and biological weapons protocols were limited to states parties to the CCW and the BTWC. That is, to negotiate in these processes a country had to be a member of its parent treaty. Despite this being a limitation in theory it appeared to impose few limits in reality because of the ability of non-member states to participate as observers. These states would not be entitled to vote if the situation arose or, indeed, be counted formally in a consensus decision. In practice, however, it ensured they had a say and could influence the process through their statements and informal interaction with other delegations. A more telling guide was the overall number of states participating actively, whether member countries or not. In this respect, few observers participated in the biological protocol drafting process and only roughly 45 member countries—about a third of the BTWC membership—turned up on a regular basis to attend the Ad Hoc Group sessions and participate in drafting.

This proportion was significantly higher in the CCW context, partly because its overall membership was much smaller (92 countries in November 2003, for instance, of which 66 participated in the 2003 meeting of states parties, which agreed the ERW protocol).[103] Nevertheless, there was considerable interest in negotiations to tackle ERW from developing countries (many of whom are ERW-affected). Despite not having acceded to the CCW, countries like the Libyan Arab Jamahiriya (an observer) and Egypt (a signatory) were active in the talks.

Disparities in state participation are most evident in comparing negotiations in the Conference on Disarmament with the United Nations Migrant Workers Convention, the FCCC and the WHO FCTC processes. Negotiation of the FCCC and the United Nations Migrant Workers Convention were open to all governments belonging to the United Nations. Similarly the WHO FCTC process was open to the entire membership of the World Health Organization.[104] By contrast, the rate of observership to the Conference on Disarmament (which has a restricted membership of 66 member states) is telling. The CD's rules of procedure effectively require non-member states to apply to the Conference for observer status on an annual basis in order to attend plenary sessions.[105] Over the last few years, since deadlock in the CD began and it has become clear that this will also prevent a widening of membership to further countries, interest in CD observership has steadily fallen.[106] This appears to be mirrored within the membership of the Conference, as member governments have, in many cases, downsized their delegations and withdrawn ambassadors for disarmament in some instances and the number of countries actively engaged in ongoing consultations has dipped.

CORE GROUPS

Results in the successful processes we have examined were characterized by core groups of like-minded delegates who:

- Provided an expert input (they were knowledgeable about the technical subject, beyond career diplomacy);
- Ensured continuity and an institutional memory, since their delegates followed the process from the beginning to the end;
- Were sufficiently small in number to be able to meet and draft between the plenary sessions; and

- Did not have preoccupying vested interests in order to remain credible.

Informal core groups helped to build up "trust" in these processes among broader participants.

NON-GOVERNMENTAL ORGANIZATION PARTICIPATION

The rules of procedure in the Conference on Disarmament place the strictest limits on NGO attendance and participation, followed by the BTWC process. NGOs attend *only* formal plenary meetings. These are usually set-piece affairs for formal statements or the gavelling in of reports in each case. There is no provision in the CD for civil society statements. NGOs may only communicate with member states through the CD secretariat.[107] On one occasion annually, on International Women's Day a joint NGO statement is delivered to the CD but must be read by the Deputy Secretary General of the Conference instead of an NGO representative.[108]

The FCCC, the WHO FCTC and the ERW protocol negotiations, in contrast, have been more open to NGO participation. The proceedings of the CCW discussions and negotiations on ERW were largely attended by NGO delegates and had the active participation also of international organizations such as the ICRC and the Mine Action Service of the United Nations. Collectively these entities made a substantial contribution. NGO participation in the WHO FCTC process was unprecedented in that NGOs were frequently (and openly) invited to informal meetings to lend their expertise and knowledge on issues under discussion.

APPOINTMENT OF OFFICE-HOLDERS

Appointment of office-holders varied in the six processes examined. For instance, Ambassador Amorim of Brazil's experience is instructive. Amorim was Chairperson of the INB in the WHO FCTC negotiations and also presided over the Conference on Disarmament during the 2000 session. In the WHO FCTC process, Ambassador Amorim was *elected* to chair the INB process. By contrast his presidency in the Conference on Disarmament was a consequence of the four-week rotational policy that is dictated by rule 9 of the CD's rules of procedure and, as noted above, allowed little time as President to foster the compromises necessary to reignite fissile negotiations through achievement of a work programme.

Although it is not uncommon for the working group chairs to rotate on the basis of regional groupings to ensure equality of representation, the chair of the Conference on Disarmament rotates every four weeks on the basis of alphabetical order. This custom is significantly different from the other five processes under consideration and would appear to make little sense beyond theoretical egalitarianism (theoretical because the body is not universal in membership). The WHO FCTC, the FCCC, the United Nations Migrant Workers Convention, the biological weapons process and ERW Protocol processes all had elected chairs. They undoubtedly benefited from this in that tenure depended to a greater extent upon merit or influence than to alphabetical geography.

Decision–Making Procedures

In all six negotiating processes it was intended that all substantive decisions be made on the basis of consensus although some—like the FCCC, WHO FCTC processes and BTWC review meetings (although not the Ad Hoc Group)—contain procedures for voting in extreme cases. Orthodox preference for consensus is for a variety of reasons: precedent, the awareness that in most cases it is important to move with the broadest possible support of the international community and, because majority voting would have been advantageous to large groups like the Group of 77 and disadvantageous to others for instance in the case of the United Nations Migrant Workers Convention.

In the security domain an argument is sometimes heard that because issues of national security (and potentially of national survival) are concerned, consensus decision-making is essential. However, history demonstrates otherwise. India and Pakistan's decisions, for example, not to join a consensus on the Comprehensive Nuclear-Test-Ban Treaty in the CD in 1996 could have scuppered a treaty widely thought to be of broader international security value at the time. A group of states took this draft instrument to the United Nations General Assembly and voted it in, belying the claim that new treaties must have international consensus before they can be agreed—at least in the CD context.

It is unlikely that mixed rules of procedure (that is, provision for voting if consensus is impossible to achieve) really have had a positive effect in promoting consensus decision-making on their own. One participant in the FCCC process noted that "the possibility of recourse to voting procedures tended to act as a restraint on influential parties and this obviated the need for actually employing the procedure".[109] But this depends on the assessments of states about whether such resort to voting will succeed. Recourse to voting was not pursued in the biological weapons process in 2001 after the United States' rejection in part because there was little appetite for agreeing a new norm in this field without that country on board.

Recourse to voting rather than consensus for decision-making carries particular risks for the birth of new disarmament and arms control multilateral norms. It is an act of political choice with serious potential consequences. Unfortunately, so is the alternative: in the CD, rule 18 of its rules of procedure has been interpreted to mean that consensus applies to all facets of the Conference's work—substantial *and* procedural. In practice member states have also taken this to mean inferring the power of veto on each of them.

GROUP INTERACTION

The presence of regional groupings in multilateral negotiations is common. Regional groups were a feature of the biological weapons and WHO FCTC processes. They meet on a regular basis in the Conference on Disarmament. Regional groups facilitate procedures such as the selection of office-holders in negotiations. They also assist in information exchange between governments and, sometimes, in the development of common positions or postures in broader multilateral settings. Moreover, regional groups constituted a mechanism for improved cohesion in the tobacco control negotiations among small states.

However, our examination has shown that regional groups can also play a spoiling role in negotiations. For instance, group cohesion became tighter in the BTWC protocol process as political polarization in the BTWC Ad Hoc Group grew from 1998, which made cross-group initiatives to build support for a robust final product more difficult. Countries supportive of robust compliance measures such as New Zealand, the Netherlands and Norway were subjected to intense pressure to cease supporting routine visit measures within the Western Group in the name of group cohesion—especially from the United States and the United Kingdom—despite this weakening the compliance goal of the negotiations. While the advantages of group cohesion in the WHO FCTC negotiations have been noted above, at the same time it sometimes led to hardening of positions, which at times stalled progress.

Regional group politics may also obscure transparency by concealing—both from members of the regional groups and from the domestic constituencies of delegations—the real nature of states' positions. This also occurred in the BTWC protocol negotiations. The United States, for instance, told other Western Group members that it opposed routine type visits to ensure confidence in compliance to relevant biological facilities (as is done under the CWC with relevant chemical facilities) because its domestic industry would not accept it and sought instead to dilute the compliance regime in later stages of drafting. However, as quoted earlier, the United States phrased this as a subsidiary argument in its public reasons for opposing a protocol on the draft instrument. In August 2001, after Ad Hoc Group negotiations began to collapse, the regional groups (including the Western Group) operated as caucuses and issued respective group statements at the conclusion of the Ad Hoc Group's last session in the hope of a successful Review Conference later that year. But on the last day of that review meeting the United States insisted on amendments concerning non-compliance and blocking a follow-on process of BTWC consultations that it could be confident would not be acceptable by consensus—amendments it did not inform its Western Group partners of beforehand.

Lack of transparency is also a factor in continuing CD deadlock because group interaction through weekly presidential consultations has become largely ritualistic and lacking in substantive engagement. The proactive ability of these CD regional groups is very limited because of cross cutting differences along alliance and nuclear-possessing versus non-nuclear-weapon states, which calls into question their utility in developing sustained and meaningful common positions.[110] By contrast, while regional groups existed in some form in the FCCC, CCW and Migrant Workers Convention settings in order to fill procedural positions and exchange information, they do not appear to have played a caucusing role.

CONCLUSIONS

This paper began by using the metaphor of cordon bleu cooking to describe the skilful process of multilateral negotiation in disarmament and arms control. In particular, this metaphor illustrates the contention central to the topic discussed; that to understand what is involved in the preparation of a fine and expensive meal it is necessary to look beyond simply the diner's expectations and examine what goes on in the kitchen. The coherency of our metaphor begins to break down as we realize that the national governments dining in this restaurant are also instrumental in that culinary preparation process. But it also illustrates that the relationship between government multilateral negotiators and their eventual products is dynamic, iterative and interactive.

Our exploration of this relationship stems from the following question: to what extent do the working practices, rules and techniques applied in multilateral disarmament and arms control contribute to or impair successful outcomes in developing or consolidating international norms? In our analysis it is apparent that, just like in a restaurant kitchen, many different dishes are prepared by a team of chefs and many supporting actors in roughly recursive—yet always at least slightly unique—operations. In other words, it is clear that a *community of practice* exists in multilateral disarmament and arms control negotiation that lends a consistency of attitude and approach between different subjects. Moreover, by comparing the CD, the BTWC process and the CCW ERW negotiations with multilateral processes outside this domain, it is clear that many, if not most, of these elements of a gradually evolving community of practice are shared more broadly, or at least have their functional equivalents.

To offer a second metaphor, it is possible to think of the community of practice in multilateral disarmament and arms control as a riverbed. The shape and course of this riverbed affects the dynamic flow of the water— the negotiating activity—within it in particular ways governed by many different factors. However, while we do not usually see it over short time frames, the water in the river gradually adjusts the shape and course of the riverbed itself by the process of erosion and so forth. The relationship between negotiating activities and their underlying community of practice is similarly dynamic.

Crucially, only part of this multilateral disarmament and arms control community of practice is "designed" in any conscious sense. Some of its manifestations are "non-designed", having developed as iterative phenomena by means of diplomatic precedent; that is, doing something again because that has been the established mode of tackling similar problems in the past. Of course, there are a number of assumptions in this—not least the perception that two problems separated in time in the real world do meaningfully lend themselves to solution by the same methods. However, at its most bare, natural scientists often strike this phenomenon—about what is functional adaptation in response to circumstances and what is not:

> Darwin himself recognized the possibility of *preadaptation*, whereby an attribute comes to serve a function which is not the reason why it was originally selected. In other words, evolution has wrought a change in function. The result may be a less than perfect instance of functional design, but evolution the tinkerer makes do. *Exaptation*, which refers to an adaptation that has recruited to some functional need a trait that either did not have any adaptive function originally or evolved for some other use, is a more recent, if not similar, formulation.[111]

There are also useful ideas here which are applicable to the processes we have analysed. The multilateral disarmament and arms control community of practice is necessarily a cautious and conservative one, as states' national security or survival may be at stake. Consequently this community of practice tends to evolve slowly. Precedent plays a major role, not least because the known practices of the past sometimes appear to provide more certainty than new and untried ones. Consensus decision-making is the ultimate comfort that a negotiating process will not move too fast or too far beyond the expectations of individual states. Because of this, some features of specific multilateral processes come about not because they were consciously and coherently designed in. Instead, they may be artefacts: features that are by-products of some other designed-in feature of an earlier or similar process, or features that have changed function through changes in patterns of usage.

Examples abound of preadaptations or exaptations in the multilateral environment. In this paper we have focused in particular on features that have pronounced consequences for the success of negotiating processes, as illustrated by our six examples. They include formal rules of procedure, the character and roles of regional groupings in different negotiations and, indeed, decision-making procedures such as the rule of consensus. As shown in the previous section, for instance, regional groupings in the BTWC and CD settings, which originated decades ago as a means of information exchange and the selection of functionaries under their formal rules of procedure, have taken on different roles for which they were not originally intended. This has been to the detriment of these processes compared with other negotiating processes, such as the CCW, climate change negotiations or the Migrant Workers Convention, in which formal regional groupings have either not existed, played a minimal role (like in the CCW) or have corresponded much more closely to the interests of their members because of the youth of these processes (the tobacco-control negotiations).

If many features of communities of practice in multilateral negotiation are not designed, but evolved through preadaptations or exaptation, it creates a number of implications invisible to orthodox explanations of political will. As explained earlier in this article and in this volume's introduction, one important reason political will is limited in its explanatory power is because it does not allow for difficulties arising in negotiations that are not products of deliberate cause. Will either exists in sufficient amounts or it does not. But as shown, this does not do justice to reality—not least to structural problems in negotiations brought about through unquestioning yielding to precedent rather than to design.

One of these implications is that the multilateral negotiating community of practice in disarmament and arms control is, at best, only partially adapted to changing realities. This is for two reasons. First, its evolution is gradual, constrained by precedent and diplomatic, political and military caution among other things. Secondly, much of its DNA is "junk DNA", consisting of features for which there is no purpose, for which a purpose has been forgotten, or which performs some function for which it was not originally developed.

In a sense, this analysis is a first, tentative attempt to sequence some of this DNA and analyse its functions. This alone is insufficient, however, without application of equivalent approaches by practitioners themselves in multilateral negotiation to their corpus of practices, attitudes and mechanisms for work. This is essential because without these insights multilateral disarmament and arms control may become doomed, by its slow rate of evolution to rapidly changing realities, to irrelevance.

Many of the elements of these new realities are intimately bound up with one another. In the introduction to this volume various facets of growing complexity were discussed, along with their implications for traditional "national security" approaches to addressing international security problems. Accompanying globalization, increased interconnectedness and new emergent problems of complexity for diplomats and national policymakers, however, has been a rise in public interest in these problems and commitment to dealing with them. As David Atwood has pointed out, "while NGO involvement in disarmament affairs is long-standing, its current manifestations are part of a broader reality of transnational civil society engagement on issues of broader concern".[112] This is also demonstrated by our three examples of climate change, migrant workers and tobacco control, in which non-governmental actors have played significant roles. In disarmament and arms control, elements of this transnational civil society, particularly the humanitarian community and its subset the humanitarian mine-action community, have performed similar roles in the context of the Antipersonnel Mine Ban Convention and the CCW. NGO engagement in small arms and light weapons issues has also been high.

Although the sample is small, the evidence suggests that multilateral negotiations not considered so intimately bound to national security imperatives—and which have been more open to civil society's involvement—have generally benefited from the expert input and energy of NGOs and other entities such as the Red Cross and Red Crescent Movement. It would be simplistic to claim that lack of progress in the CD and BTWC is due to their greater exclusion of non-governmental entities as their problems are more complex. But the coincidence is striking, as is the fact that "the official relationship between multilateral disarmament institutions and NGOs is badly out of tune with current realities in international relations and with current needs. New approaches are necessary".[113]

A number of participants from the Mine Ban Convention negotiations, including governmental representatives involved, have argued that it benefited from greater civil society involvement.[114] If one were to sum up the many different specific roles such entities can play, it could be described as making a negotiating environment more information rich, which benefits governmental negotiators directly in their decision-making.[115] With outmoded group structures, lack of trust and lack of public transparency and no substantive negotiation completed since the CTBT in the mid-1990s it would be difficult to describe the CD as information rich.

Overall, there is no simple answer to what extent working practices, rules and techniques applied in multilateral disarmament and arms control contribute to or alleviate successful negotiating outcomes. But of the three processes discussed in detail here (the CD, BTWC and CCW) alongside the three multilateral comparisons further afield (climate change, migrant workers and tobacco control) there is much food for thought. In our view:

- Multilateral disarmament and arms control negotiating processes would benefit from less emphasis on diplomatic precedent and more from focus on object-oriented processes—the object in question being security or some specific aspect thereof.
- Doing so may best entail enlisting the assistance of dedicated professionals (such as management theorists and organizational psychologists) to help in designing the architecture of their negotiating processes.
- Negotiators need to ask, individually and collectively, the following questions on a regular basis: was this feature of our community of practice designed for a good reason? Does that good reason still apply or has it changed or lost currency?
- The imposition of a rule of consensus at all stages of a process—for instance on agreeing a programme of work or to begin a negotiation that will later need consensus for agreement—as well as the value of current regional groupings need particular scrutiny in this regard.
- Experience indicates that disarmament and arms control processes flounder if they lack clear goals and objectives. Clear goals and objectives are an aid to effective leadership. To this end, opportunities for course correction are advisable (for instance, by means of changes to mandates, changing of elected office-holders, review of procedural rules) at regular intervals. The CCW ERW protocol process was a positive example in this regard. It is possible that the BTWC protocol drafting process might have been salvaged had there been a review of its mandate and progress that led to an adapted process better reflecting international realities at an earlier stage in its negotiation, for instance through a Special Conference in the late 1990s.

The challenge for multilateral disarmament and arms control is to remain relevant to solving international security problems effectively. To do so, it will need to learn to adapt quickly enough to changing circumstances. Increasing global interconnectivity, blurring distinctions in sovereignty with attendant implications for "national security" and complexity, mean that this rate of change is not going to slow any time soon.

An important step in the process of learning to adapt better to new disarmament and arms control challenges for negotiating practitioners will mean cultivating a greater willingness to try new methods and approaches they have not deployed before. Honest self-reflection of the contents of their current toolbox should demonstrate that many of its elements are not right for the job. New partners and perspectives, from transnational civil society, for instance, as well as broader recognition of the interrelationship of national security with other dimensions of human welfare (human security) can help here.

Notes

[1]   The term "disarmament" traditionally refers to the elimination, as well as the limitation or reduction (through negotiation of an international agreement) of the means by which nations wage war. The term "arms control" was coined in the 1950s to denote an international agreement to limit the arms race, in particular the nuclear arms race between the United States and the Soviet Union, following recognition that general and complete nuclear disarmament would not be readily achieved. Arms control originally was meant to denote internationally agreed rules limiting the arms competition rather than reversing it; it had a connotation distinct from the reduction or elimination of armaments (i.e. disarmament). See Robert H. Mathews and Timothy L. H. McCormack, "The Influence of Humanitarian Principles in the Negotiations of Arms Control Treaties", International Review of the Red Cross, No. 834, 1999, pp. 331-352.
The term "non-proliferation" refers to containing of the spread of weapons from states that possess them to states that do not.

[2]   The Conference on Disarmament briefly began negotiations on a fissile material treaty at the end of 1998. However the mandate for the ad hoc committee was not renewed the following year.

[3]   Also known as the Biological Weapons Convention (BWC).

[4]   The full title of the treaty is the 1980 Convention on Prohibitions or Restrictions on the Use of Certain Conventional Weapons Which May

Be Deemed to Be Excessively Injurious or to Have Indiscriminate Effects (1980).

5   The Convention on the Prohibition of the Use, Stockpiling, Production and Transfer of Anti-Personnel Mines and on their Destruction (1997). The Antipersonnel Mine Ban Convention is sometimes referred to as the Ottawa treaty, where it was signed. Final negotiations for the treaty were held in Oslo in July of that year.

6   A. Carter, *Success and Failure in Arms Control Negotiations*, Stockholm International Peace Research Institute, New York: Oxford University Press, 1989, p. 2.

7   United States Under-Secretary of State for Arms Control and International Security, John Bolton, *Statement to the Fifth Review Conference of the Biological Weapons Convention*, Geneva, December 2001, p. 2, www.opbw.org.

8   Issues related to political will are discussed in more detail earlier in this volume in the paper by John Borrie entitled "An Introduction to Disarmament as Humanitarian Action".

9   Ron Scollon, *Mediated Discourse as Social Interaction : A Study of News Discourse,* Boston: Addison Wesley, 1998, pp. 12-13.

10 The authors wish to thank Mr Juhanni Lönnroth, currently the Director General of the European Commission Directorate General for Translation, for his assistance. Mr Lönnroth was actively involved in the negotiations of the United Nations International Convention on Migrant Workers and Their Families—first as a participant and later as vice-chairman of the Working Group. Mr Lönnroth was also spokesman for the MESCA group.

11 See S. Hune and J. Niessen, "The First UN Convention on Migrant Workers", *Netherlands Quarterly of Human Rights,* Vol. 9, 1991, No. 2, p. 132 for a more detailed commentary.

12 The ILO is a specialized agency of the United Nations. It has a unique tripartite structure in which employers' and workers' representatives are on an equal footing with governments. The ILO sets minimum labour standards. The broad policies of the ILO are set by the International Labour Conference, which meets annually.

13 United Nations Economic and Social Council, Commission on Human Rights Sub-Commission on Prevention of Discrimination and Protection of Minorities, Twenty-eighth session, Item 8 of the provisional agenda, "Exploitation of Labour Through Illicit and Clandestine Trafficking", E/CN.4/Sub.2/L.629, 4 July 1975.

14 Hune and Niessen, op. cit.

15   Vanessa Martin Randin's interview with Juhanni Lönnroth, 27 August 2004.

16   J. Lönnroth, "United Nations Convention: An Analysis of Ten Years of Negotiations", *International Migration Review*, Vol. 25, No. 96, Winter 1991, p. 724.

17   The four Mediterranean states were Greece, Italy, Portugal and Spain and the three Scandinavian states were Finland, Sweden and Norway.

18   United Nations General Assembly resolution A/RES/45/158.

19   For a more in-depth discussion see Lönnroth, op. cit., pp. 716-721.

20   R. Böhning, "The ILO and the New UN Convention on Migrant Workers", *International Migration Review*, Vol. 25, No. 96, Winter 1991, p. 702.

21   Taken from the report of the Economic and Social Council, 1981b, pp. 2-3, which outlines the philosophy and approach underpinning the MESCA proposals.

22   Böhning, op. cit., p. 702.

23   The authors thank Dr Brook Boyer of the United Nations Institute for Training and Research (UNITAR) and Ambassador Bo Kjellèn of Sweden for their assistance.

24   P. S. Chasek, *Earth Negotiations: Analyzing Thirty Years of Environmental Diplomacy*, United Nations University, 2001, p. 124.

25   INC 1 in Chantilly VA, near Washington, DC in February 1991; INC 2 in Geneva, Switzerland from 19 to 28 June 1991; INC 3 in Nairobi from 9 to 20 September 1991; INC 4 in Geneva from 9 to 20 December 1991; INC 5 in New York from February to May 1992.

26   D. Bodansky, "Prologue to the Climate Convention" in I. Minter and J. A. Leonard (eds), *Negotiating Climate Change: The Inside Story of the Rio Convention*, Cambridge: Cambridge University Press, 1994, p. 63.

27   Prior to his election to the post of Chairman of the FCCC INC negotiations in 1991 Ripert was Director General of Economic Affairs at the United Nations in New York.

28   The Extended Bureau contained office-holders in the negotiations (members of its formal, elected General Committee) and other "Friends of the Chair". Many multilateral negotiations establish this general type of group at some point. It may be known by different names, depending on political sensitivities. The "Friends of the Chair" (or the extended bureau in the case of the FCCC) was a small group of delegates representing the main interest groups and key delegations that met privately with the Chair to provide views and advice.

See J. Delpedge, *Organizing Successful Negotiations for the FCTC: Options and Lessons From Other Conventions*, London: Action on Smoking and Health (ASH), 8 October 2001, http://www.ash.org.uk/html/international/html/negotiatingprocess.html.

The FCCC Extended Bureau comprised the chair of the Group of 77, the President of the European Union and key players like the United States, China, India, Brazil, Japan and the Russian Federation.

29 D. Bodansky, "The United Nations Framework Convention on Climate Change: A Commentary", *The Yale Journal of International Law*, Vol. 18, Summer 1993, p. 491.

30 D. Bodansky, "Prologue to the Climate Convention", p. 69.

31 Under Article 7(2) of the FCCC the "Conference of Parties as the supreme body of the Convention shall keep under regular review, the implementation of the Convention and any related legal instruments that the Conference of Parties may adopt, and shall move, within its mandate, the decisions necessary to promote the effective improvement of the Convention".

32 Article 9 of the FCCC established a subsidiary body for scientific and technological advice. Article 10 established a subsidiary body for implementation.

33 Chasek, op. cit., p. 132.

34 The entry into force of the Kyoto Protocol had been dependent on the Russian Federation since the United States had withdrawn its signature in 2001. The ratification procedure required the signature of at least 55 parties to the Convention. This needed to include enough Annex 1 parties (industrialized nations) to account for at least 55% of total CO_2 emissions from industrialized countries in 1990. The Russian Federation ratified the Kyoto Protocol on 22 October 2004. The entry into force provision of the Protocol was triggered when the Russian Federation deposited its instrument of ratification with the treaty's depository—the Secretary-General of the United Nations—on 19 November 2004. The Protocol officially enters into force after 90 days, i.e. on 19 February 2005.

35 Chasek, op. cit., p. 127.

36 In a personal assessment of the FCCC negotiations, Bo Kjellen described Ripert's approach: "I believe that style certainly plays an important role for a chairman—and Jean Ripert's style certainly fit the challenges of this negotiation. Most of the time he acted with an almost palpable slowness: but this was on the surface. While explaining technical or legal details pertaining to the negotiation in painstaking

(some would say irritating) detail, his mind was searching out solutions and anticipating ways to avoid blocked solutions. It became clear that this was his method of work. The overall effect inspired broad confidence in his leadership. In the final stages, when heads of key delegations were invited by the chairman to negotiate the final texts and thrash out the last difficulties, we were all impressed by the sharpness of the picture he laid out before us. Ripert's leadership style did not exclude the human touch. He was able to remind the negotiators of the real issues beyond the drafting and of their responsibility to the international community without sounding condescending or offensive." B. Kjellen, "A Personal Assessment", in I. Minter and J. A. Leonard (eds), *Negotiating Climate Change: The Inside Story of the Rio Convention,* Cambridge: Cambridge University Press, 1994, p. 153.

[37] A. Djoghlaf, "The Beginnings of International Climate Law", in I. Minter and J. A. Leonard (eds), *Negotiating Climate Change: The Inside Story of the Rio Convention,* Cambridge: Cambridge University Press, 1994, p. 103.

[38] NGO participation in the FCCC plenary meetings extended to their participation as observers in the actual negotiations of the FCCC text.

[39] A. Rahman and A. Ronceral, "A View from the Ground Up", I. Minter and J. A. Leonard (eds), *Negotiating Climate Change: The Inside Story of the Rio Convention,* Cambridge: Cambridge University Press, 1994, p. 240.

[40] CAN exploited the influence of *ECO* particularly effectively in INC 2, in which technology cooperation and transfer was the main topic of discussion. Discussions at this meeting focused specifically on a non-paper on this topic by the United States. A series of other non-papers circulated by the United Kingdom, France, Japan, Sweden, Australia and New Zealand explored the topic of "pledge and review", whereby states would pledge their commitment to greenhouse gas reductions without undertaking specific legal obligations. However there was no consensus on whether or not the pledge would include global targets, commitments or minimum actions. India rejected the "pledge and review" idea on grounds that it would give countries an excuse not to make solid commitments to reduce greenhouse gas emissions and therefore would be ineffective. This position received publicity and vociferous support from members of CAN, via *ECO* (labelling the "pledge and review" approach "hedge and retreat"), and also by

various developing countries. As a result the "pledge and review" concept was eventually seen off.

41 S. Mori, *What is the Missing Link? Multilateral Environmental Governance, Regimes, Structural Integration and the Possibility of a World Environment Organization,* International Environmental Governance, Gaps and Weaknesses/Proposals for Reform, Working Paper, Tokyo, UNU/IAS, 2002.

42 The authors are grateful to the Framework Convention Team for the Tobacco-Free Initiative at the WHO, particularly Dr Douglas Bettcher, Ms Marta Seoane and Ms Gemma Vestal for their time and assistance.

43 Intergovernmental Negotiating Body on the WHO Framework Convention on Tobacco Control (First session, Provisional agenda item 4), *Secretariat Update: Provisional timetable for the negotiating process and provisional costs,* A/FCTC/INB1/3, 5 September 2000.

44 A. L. Taylor and D. W. Bettcher, "WHO Framework Convention on Tobacco Control: A Global 'Good' for Public Health", *Bulletin of the World Health Organization,* No. 78 (7), 2000, p. 923.

45 These public hearing were attended by academics, NGOs and others in the FCTC process. Although the summary records of the hearings were not official, the NGO community used the information to develop their platform for lobbying governments at later stages of the process.

46 "Participation of Non-Governmental Organizations in Official or Provisional Official Relations with WHO in the Open-Ended Intergovernmental Working Group on the WHO Framework Convention on Tobacco Control", 20 May 2000, Open-ended Intergovernmental Working Group on the WHO Framework Convention on Tobacco Control, A/FCTC/IGWG/1/DIV/3.

47 The Framework Convention Alliance claims it drew inspiration from the NGO coalition-building experiences of the International Campaign to Ban Landmines (ICBL). For further discussion of the NGO mobilization in the FCTC experience see: Infact, "Mobilizing NGOs and the Media Behind the International Framework Convention on Tobacco Control", Technical Briefing Series, Paper 3, 1999, Tobacco Free Initiative and World Health Organization, WHO/NCD/TFI/99.3. This is available online at http://whqlibdoc.who.int./hq/1999/WHO_NCD_TFI_99.3.pdf.

48 *After the first negotiating session*, intersessional consultations were hosted by South Africa (African region) and by Indonesia (South-East Asian region); *after the second negotiating session*, intersessional

meetings were hosted by Algeria (African region), Bhutan (South-East Asian region), Estonia (Baltic states), Iran (Eastern Mediterranean region), New Zealand (Pacific Island) and the Russian Federation (Commonwealth of Independent States (CIS)); *after the third negotiating session*, intersessional consultations were hosted by India (South-East Asian region), Côte d'Ivoire (African region), Egypt (Eastern Mediterranean region), Peru (Latin American and Caribbean Group (GRULAC) and Malaysia (Association of South-East Asian Nations (ASEAN). Additionally an Interministerial Conference was held in Warsaw; *after the fourth negotiating session*, intersessional meetings were hosted by New Caledonia (Pacific Island region), Myanmar (South-East Asian region), Bulgaria (South-Eastern European countries), Thailand (ASEAN), Malawi (African region), Russian Federation (CIS), Estonia (Baltic states), Mexico (GRULAC), Bahrain (Eastern Mediterranean region) and Denmark (European region). Additionally an international conference on illicit tobacco trade was held at United Nations Headquarters in New York from 30 July to 1 August 2002).

49 G. Jacob, "Perspectives: Without Reservation", *Chicago Journal of International Law*, No. 281, Summer 2004, pp. 287-302.

50 World Health Organization, *The Framework Convention on Tobacco Control: A Primer*, A/FCTC/INB2/2 of 2003, pp. 8-9.

51 Amorim was posted to London as Ambassador in November 2001. Since then he has become Brazil's Foreign Minister.

52 BBC World News, "Key Anti-Smoking Treaty adopted" (available online at <http://news.bbc.co.uk/1/hi/health/3046223.stm> (21 May 2003).

53 Jacob, op. cit. Gregory F. Jacob described some of the tactics he alleged that certain NGOs present at the FCTC negotiations resorted to: "Much of the information distributed by the NGOs was valuable and accurate, but some NGOs were not above stooping to underhanded and manipulative tactics. For example, during INB5 I had to file a complaint with the WHO Secretariat when I caught members of Infact deliberately attempting to listen in on a private cell phone conversation I was having with the White House. I received the call while I was in the main negotiation chamber and left the room so that I could talk freely without disturbing others and without being overheard. As I left the room with the phone to my ear, however, a member of Infact began to tail me, forcing me to move into a narrow corridor where it would be difficult to follow me inconspicuously. I finished my conversation from an alcove just off the corridor, only to

find as I emerged at the end of my call that another Infact member had been sent through the corridor from the opposite direction and was kneeling down around the corner, studiously taking notes."

54   Infact, *Cowboy Diplomacy: How the US undermines International Environmental, Human Rights, Disarmament and Health Agreements,* http://www.infact.org/cowboyd.html.

55   Jacob, op. cit.

56   The FCTC entered into force on 27 February 2005 less than two years after it opened for signature.

57   *NGOs Applaud Commitment of Developing Nations to Comprehensive Advertising Ban in Final Round of Treaty Talks,* Network of Accountability of Tobacco Transnationals (NATT), 21 February 2003.

58   Böhning, op. cit., p. 701.

59   See S. Tulliu and T. Schmalberger, *Coming to Terms With Security: A Lexicon for Arms Control, Disarmament and Confidence-Building,* UNIDIR, Geneva: United Nations, 2001, pp. 177-178. The Conference on Disarmament succeeded the Ten-Nation Committee on Disarmament (1959-1960), the Eighteen-Nation Committee on Disarmament (1962-1969), the Conference of the Committee on Disarmament (1969-1978) and the Committee on Disarmament (1979-1983).

60   New Zealand Ministry of Foreign Affairs and Trade, *United Nations Handbook 2002,* Wellington, New Zealand: PrintLink, p. 33.

61   Rules of procedure of the Conference on Disarmament, CD/8/Rev.8, 17 August 1999.

62   The division of the annual session is outlined in Rule 7 of the CD rules of procedure: "The Conference shall have an annual session divided into three parts of 10 weeks, 7 weeks and 7 weeks respectively. The first part shall begin the penultimate week of the month of January. The Conference shall decide the actual dates of the three parts of its annual session at the close of the previous year's session. The President of the Conference, in full consultation with and with the agreement of all its members, may convene the Conference in special session."

63   Rule 13 of the CD's rules of procedure states: "At the request of the Conference the Secretary-General of the United Nations, following consultations with the Conference, will appoint the Secretary-General of the Conference, who shall also act as his personal representative, to assist the Conference and its president in organizing the business and timetables of the Conference." Rules 14-17 of the CD's rules of procedure outline the duties of the Secretary-General of the CD.

Sergei Ordzhonikidze of the Russian Federation has been the Secretary-General of the CD since 20 March 2002.

64 This derives from rule 9 of the CD rules of procedure. It is not unknown for states to stand aside from the Presidency, however. Iran decided to forgo its turn at the Presidency at the beginning of 2003, for instance. The next country alphabetically, Iraq, notified the CD that it would do the same on 3 February 2003.

65 The CD membership increased from 31 to 40 states in 1978. After Germany's reunification in 1990 this number fell to 39 and then to 38 with the break-up of Czechoslovakia. In 1996 the CD decided to admit 23 new members. However since this number included Iraq, a state under United Nations sanctions for its act of aggression against Kuwait, a caveat was applied to their admittance. In a joint letter to the President of the Conference the 23 had to commit not to obstruct any action of the Conference by resorting to the rule of consensus. "This commitment would cease to apply if a consensus decision were reached in the CD that the 'circumstance' which had given rise to the situation requiring it no longer existed. For any of the new members not subject to comprehensive enforcement measures under Chapter VII of the United Nations Charter, the above commitment would cease to apply two years after the decision to enlarge the CD had been adopted." See J. Goldblat, *Arms Control: The New Guide to Negotiations and Agreements*, International Peace Research Institute (PRIO), Oslo: Sage Publications, 2002, p. 14.

66 The 66 members of the CD are: Algeria, Argentina, Australia, Austria, Bangladesh, Belarus, Belgium, Brazil, Bulgaria, Cameroon, Canada, Chile, China, Columbia, Cuba, Democratic People's Republic of Korea, Democratic Republic of the Congo, Ecuador, Egypt, Ethiopia, Finland, France, Germany, Hungary, India, Indonesia, Iran, Iraq, Ireland, Israel, Italy, Japan, Kazakhstan, Kenya, Malaysia, Mexico, Mongolia, Morocco, Myanmar, Netherlands, New Zealand, Nigeria, Norway, Pakistan, Peru, Poland, Republic of Korea, Romania, Russian Federation, Senegal, Slovakia, South Africa, Spain, Sri Lanka, Sweden, Switzerland, Syrian Arab Republic, Tunisia, Turkey, Ukraine, United Kingdom of Great Britain and Northern Ireland, United States of America, Venezuela, Vietnam, Zimbabwe.

67 Under rule 42, "All communications from non-governmental organizations to the Conference, to the President or to the Secretariat, shall be retained by the Secretariat and be made available to

delegations upon request. A list of all such communication shall be circulated to the Conference."

[68] J. Goldblat, "The Conference on Disarmament at the Crossroads: To Revitalize or Dissolve?", *The Non-proliferation Review*, Summer 2000, Vol. 2, No. 9, pp. 104-107, p. 105.

[69] Document CD/WP.533.

[70] Rule 28 of the CD rules of procedure. (CD/8/Rev.8).

[71] Ibid., Rule 29.

[72] Ibid., Rule 19. The rules of procedure are vague on whether informal and subsidiary body meetings may be open to non-state actors. Historically they have been closed.

[73] This is in line with Rule 23 of the CD rules of procedure (CD/8/Rev.8).

[74] "Mandate for an Ad Hoc Committee under Agenda Item 1: "Nuclear Test Ban", document CD/1238, 25 January 1994.

[75] No definition of fissile material has yet been drawn up for fissile negotiations. However, fissile material is commonly considered to include plutonium (Pu) and highly-enriched uranium (HEU)—that is, uranium containing 20% or more of the fissile isotope uranium-235. At least three other types of fissile material are relevant to fissile negotiations : uranium-232 (which arises from the irradiation of thorium-232 in a nuclear reactor, neptunium-237 (produced by neutron capture when uranium-235 is irradiated) and americium-241 (a decay product of plutonium-241). Tritium, an isotope of hydrogen sometimes utilized by nuclear-weapon designers to boost the explosive yield of fissile weapons, is not a fissile material. See William Walker and Frans Berkhout, *Fissile Material Stocks: Characteristics, Measures and Policy Options*, UNIDIR, Geneva: United Nations, 1999.

[76] The five Ambassadors were Mohamed Salah Dembri of Algeria, Jean Lint of Belgium, Camilo Reyes of Colombia, Henrik Salander of Sweden and Juan Enrique Vega of Chile.

[77] The Shannon Report called for the negotiation of a non-discriminatory, multilateral and internationally and effectively verifiable treaty banning the production of fissile material for nuclear weapons or other nuclear explosive devices.

[78] The expert briefings took place within the context of the regional group meetings and other ad hoc informal gatherings. Only member states of the CD were permitted to attend the presentation given by the experts.

[79] See Clifford E. Singer and Amy Sands, *Keys to Unblocking Multilateral Nuclear Arms Control*, ACDIS Occasional Paper, University of Illinois at Urbana-Champaign: ACDIS, July 2002, p. 3.

80   Article I of the BTWC states that, " Each State Party to this Convention undertakes never in any circumstances to develop, produce, stockpile or otherwise acquire or retain: (1) microbial or other biological agents, or toxins whatever their origin or method of production, of types and in quantities that have no justification for prophylactic, protective or other peaceful purposes; (2) weapons, equipment or means of delivery designed to use such agents or toxins for hostile purposes or in armed conflict." Moreover, Article III states that "Each State Party to this Convention undertakes not to transfer to any recipient whatsoever, directly or indirectly, and not in any way to assist, encourage, or induce any State, group of States or international organizations to manufacture or otherwise acquire any of the agents, toxins, weapons, equipment or means of delivery specified in Article I of the Convention."

81   Arms Control and Disarmament Research Unit, *Chemical Weapons Convention Negotiations 1972-92*, Foreign Policy Document No. 243, Foreign and Commonwealth Office, England: C.W. Print Group, 1993, pp. 4-6.

82   For a more in-depth discussion of the Biological Weapons Programmes of South Africa, see C. Gould and P. Folb, *Project Coast: Apartheid's Chemical and Biological Warfare Programme*, UNIDIR, Geneva: United Nations, 2002.

83   Review meetings are convened roughly every five years. The last, in December 2001, was suspended and reconvened in December 2002. Under the BTWC Review Conference rules of procedure (BWC/CONF.V/17) signatories to the Convention are allowed to participate in proceedings but cannot take part in the adoption of decisions. Participation of NGOs in the review process is limited; NGOs can only receive documents from the Conference by request, although they have usually been allowed access to plenary meetings at the commencement and conclusion of Review Conferences.

84   Ad Hoc Group of Governmental Experts to Identify and Examine Potential Verification Measures from a Scientific and Technical Standpoint, summary report, (BWC/CONF.III/VEREX/9) (Geneva, 24 September 1993).

85   J. P. Zanders et al., Chemical and Biological Weapon Developments and Arms Control, *SIPRI Yearbook*, 2002, Oxford: Oxford University Press, 2002, p. 667.

86   Final Declaration of the Final Document of the Fourth Review Conference of the Parties to the Convention on the Prohibition of the Development, Production and Stockpiling of Bacteriological and Toxin

Weapons and their Destruction (BWC/CONF.IV/9), Geneva, 1996, p. 29, http://www.opbw.org/rev_cons/4rc/docs/final_dec/4RC_final_dec.pdf.

87 For a useful perspective on this from an individual who had seen both UNSCOM inspection service in Iraq, had experience of the Trilateral Inspections as well as the Ad Hoc Group negotiations, see David C. Kelly, "Verification of Compliance with the Biological Weapons Convention" in *Changing Threats to Global Security: Peace or Turmoil*, Proceedings of the XV International Amaldi Conference, 2003, Helsinki, Delegation of the Finnish Academies of Science and Letters, 2003, pp. 227-242. This article was authorized by his widow and is based on a presentation he delivered at the Amaldi Conference not long before his tragic death.

88 This was always a perceived group with a fluid membership over time. It usually included Iran, the Libyan Arab Jamahiriya, Cuba, India, Pakistan and China.

89 Ambassador Donald Mahley, (United States Special Negotiator for Chemical and Biological Arms Control Issues), statement by the United States to the Ad Hoc Group of Biological Weapons Convention States Parties, Geneva, 25 July 2001.

90 Statement of the Honourable John R. Bolton, Under-Secretary of State for Arms Control and International Security, United States Department of States to the Fifth Review Conference of the Biological Weapons Convention, Geneva, 19 November 2001, http://www.us-mission.ch/press2001/1911bolton.htm.

91 Rule 28 of the Review Conference rules of procedure states that a two-thirds majority vote can be taken on an issue of substance if all efforts at consensus have been exhausted. See also Nicholas A. Sims, "Biological Disarmament Diplomacy in the Doldrums: Reflections After the BWC Fifth Review Conference", *Disarmament Diplomacy*, No. 70, April- May 2003.

92 The CCW scope operates differently from some other treaties in the arms control or humanitarian spheres. To become a state party to the CCW a state must ratify the framework Convention and a minimum of two of its Protocols. However, a state party is not compelled to ratify new (that is, more than two) Protocols to remain a member of the treaty under its current rules.

93 These include: (1) the requirement that a distinction be made at all times between civilians and combatants; and (2) the prohibition of the use of weapons which inflict excessive injury or suffering on

combatants or render their death inevitable. "While these general principles apply to all weapons used in armed conflict, the Convention imposes specific prohibitions or restrictions on the use of conventional weapons about which there is widespread concern", International Committee 'of the Red Cross, Convention on Prohibitions or Restrictions on the Use of Certain Conventional Weapons Which May Be Deemed to Be Excessively Injurious or to Have Indiscriminate Effects, ICRC, June 2004, p. 6.

94 Protocol on Blinding Laser Weapons (Protocol IV to the 1980 Convention), 13 October 1995.

95 When these discussions began, no consensus definition existed of "explosive remnants of war". Over the course of CCW work a general working understanding developed that this term covered munitions that had failed to function as intended in conflict and abandoned munitions but not anti-personnel mines or "mines other than anti-personnel mines". In the final text of the ERW protocol "Explosive remnants of war means unexploded ordnance and abandoned explosive ordnance".

96 See the International Committee of the Red Cross report, *Expert Meeting on Explosive Remnants of War : A Summary Report*, Nyon, Switzerland, 18-19 September 2002. This meeting was organized around four main subjects: (1) the humanitarian impact of submunitions and other unexploded ordnance in various contexts ; (2) related technical issues ; (3) the use and military utility of cluster bomb submunitions ; and (4) possible measures to address the problem of explosive remnants of war.

97 The United Nations General Assembly had passed resolution 55/37 at its fifty-fifth session on 20 November 2000, calling on states parties to convene the next Review Conference not later than 2001.

98 "In case of armed conflicts not of an international character occurring in the territory of one of the High Contracting Parties, each party to the conflict shall be bound to apply the prohibitions and restrictions of this Convention and its annexed Protocols." See the Convention on Prohibitions or Restrictions on the Use of Certain Conventional Weapons Which May Be Deemed to Be Excessively Injurious or to Have Indiscriminate Effects, Geneva, 10 October 1980. Amendment to Article 1, 21 December 2001.

99 See the draft report of the meeting of the states parties to the Convention on Prohibitions or Restrictions on the Use of Certain Conventional Weapons Which May Be Deemed to Be Excessively

Injurious or to Have Indiscriminate effects, CCW/MSP/2002/CRP.1, Geneva, 12-13 December 2002.

[100] Protocol on Explosive Remnants of War (Protocol V to the 1980 Convention), 28 November 2003.

[101] Report of the Second Review Conference of the States Parties to the *Convention on Prohibitions or Restrictions on the Use of Certain Conventional Weapons Which May Be Deemed to Be Excessively Injurious or to Have Indiscriminate Effects*, Geneva, 21 December 2001, http://www.ccwtreaty.com/report.htm.

[102] CCW Protocol V will enter into force for states that have acceded to that legal instrument when 20 countries have acceded.

[103] See the report of the states parties to the *Convention on Prohibitions or Restrictions on the Use of Certain Conventional Weapons Which May Be Deemed to Be Excessively Injurious or to Have Indiscriminate Effects*, CCW/MSP/2003/3, Geneva, 16 February 2004.

[104] The United Nations has a membership of 191 members while the World Health Organization's membership stands at 192 states.

[105] Rule 32 of the CD rules of procedure (CD/8/Rev.8) states: "Representatives of non-member states shall have reserved seats in the conference room during plenary meeting and, if the Conference so decides, at other meetings." Application of non-member countries to attend must then be adopted by consensus by the member states of the Conference. Rule 33 of the rules of procedure does, however, allow for "non-member states to submit written proposals or working documents on measures of disarmament that are the subject of negotiation in the Conference". According to Rule 34 non-member states may also be invited to express their views to the Conference upon request.

[106] Between 1998 and 2004, for instance, the list of countries with observer status in the CD fell from 47 to 38. (This actually reflects a slight rise from 2002 and 2003 when it fell to a low of 37.)

[107] Rule 42 of the CD rules of procedure (CD/8/Rev.8).

[108] See, for instance, the 2003 Joint NGO statement to the Conference on Disarmament read by the Deputy-Secretary General of the Conference on Disarmament, Enrique Roman-Morey, http://www.wilpf.int.ch/disarmament/cd2003.htm.

[109] C. Dasgupta, "Prologue to the Climate Convention", in I. Minter and J. A. Leonard (eds), *Negotiating Climate Change: The Inside Story of the Rio Convention*, Cambridge: Cambridge University Press, 1994, p. 132.

[110] Of the 22 members of the Western Group three states (France, United Kingdom and United States) are nuclear-weapon states and also members of the North Atlantic Treaty Organisation (NATO). Israel is believed to possess nuclear weapons also. Ten of the 22 (Belgium, Canada, Germany, Hungary, Italy, Netherlands, Norway, Poland, Spain and Turkey are also members of NATO). Only Austria, Australia, Ireland, Israel, Japan, New Zealand, the Republic of Korea and Sweden are not NATO members in the Western Group, although some have bilateral defence treaties with at least one nuclear-weapon state. Out of the 31 states that officially comprise the Non-Aligned Movement in the CD, India and Pakistan possess nuclear weapons and the Democratic People's Republic of Korea and Iran may be—or may be on the road to being—nuclear capable. Of the states that comprise the Group of Eastern States in the CD one, the Russian Federation, is a nuclear-weapon state, while Bulgaria and Romania are members of NATO. Only Belarus and Ukraine are non-NATO members. As mentioned, China stands outside the group system by choice and is also a nuclear-weapon state.

[111] Henry Plotkin, *The Imagined World Made Real: Towards a Natural Science of Culture*, London: Penguin, 2002, p. 34. Italics inserted by the authors.

[112] David C. Atwood, "NGOs and Disarmament: Views from the Coal Face", *Disarmament Forum*, UNIDIR, Geneva: United Nations, No. 1, 2002, pp. 5-14, p. 6.

[113] Ibid., p. 9.

[114] See Don Hubert, *The Landmine Ban: A Case Study in Humanitarian Advocacy*, Occasional Paper No. 42, Thomas J. Watson Jr. Institute for International Studies, 2000.

[115] These roles include generating public awareness, constituency-building and campaigning at the national and transnational levels, "reframing" issues, policy-agenda building and policy development, developing and changing norms, lobby/advocacy, exchanging and targeting of information, researching and expert policy advising, monitoring and evaluating actor behaviour, developing "track II" initiatives and implementing policy.

Some alternative approaches in multilateral decision making: disarmament as humanitarian action

Wednesday 3 November 2004, Room IX, Palais des Nations, Geneva, 13:00-17:00

Summary of discussions

INTRODUCTION

Multilateral disarmament and arms control negotiation processes have experienced limited success in recent years. In recognizing the need for innovative approaches to reinvigorate multilateral efforts, the United Nations Institute for Disarmament Research (UNIDIR) recently launched a project entitled "Disarmament as Humanitarian Action: Making Multilateral Negotiations Work". This project is producing research with a view to coming up with new tools for multilateral decision-making processes. UNIDIR hosted a conference on 3 November 2004 at the Palais des Nations in Geneva to introduce the project and present some initial ideas on the following themes:

1. The relevance of humanitarian and "human security" perspectives to moving the arms control and disarmament agenda forward;
2. The arms control and disarmament negotiating machinery, its procedures and working practice.

HUMANITARIAN PERSPECTIVES AND DISARMAMENT AND ARMS CONTROL NEGOTIATIONS

The meeting's presenters observed that the arms control and disarmament community has been slow to adapt to the increasing complexity and interconnectedness of the current international security environment. The concept of "human security" has merits in constructively linking disarmament to an array of disciplines that are often neglected in

131

traditional state security discussions. For instance, "public health" perspectives had relevance to arms control and disarmament processes, as shown by the work of the World Health Organization (WHO) and the International Committee of the Red Cross (ICRC) in understanding armed violence as a health problem.

Various difficulties were noted in using differing conceptions of "human security" in arms control and disarmament. These included problems of definition, and reluctance by some governments to lend credence to an approach they fear might undermine national security concerns. Moreover, it was noted that the international direction since the 11 September 2001 attacks and the prosecution of the subsequent "war on terror" had seen human security sidelined to some extent. Good work had been done using human security concepts, however, including the Commission on Sovereignty's work on the "responsibility to protect". The upcoming report of the United Nations High Level Panel on Threats, Challenges and Threats was also expected to be interesting in this regard.

Despite these challenges in "operationalizing" humanitarian and human security concepts into multilateral negotiators' practice, several of the panelists stressed the need for work in this area. Bridging this divide, it was thought by the panelists, would help in linking individual rights, humanitarianism and disarmament in beneficial ways. One participant also noted subtle differences between the use of "human security" and terms such as "humanitarianism"; the latter sometimes criticized for assuming moral high ground in complex human situations. At the same time, orthodox, realist notions of "national" or "state" security were, alone, increasingly insufficient on their own to tackle increasingly complex and multifaceted security problems. "Human security" could have utility, therefore, in allowing discourse in disarmament and arms control to have a more objective basis on which to assess issues of international security.

RE-EVALUATING THE MULTILATERAL NEGOTIATING MACHINERY

The importance of existing multilateral negotiating machinery to the practice of effective negotiation was discussed at length, especially explanations for difficulties in terms of insufficient political will. A range of views emerged. A few participants argued that specific methods and practices are of little or no consequence to the outcome of negotiations. Instead, success is dependent on the desire of all participants to achieve a positive result. Others argued that such explanations couched in terms of political will have limited explanatory power at best, and are often tautologies. Political will was not necessarily definable or distinct from the processes it apparently infused. Nor did participants agree on whether or how political will could be generated in the midst of a negotiating process. If political will could not be defined except by its perceived effects then it was difficult to tell whether political was all that was necessary, or whether other factors, such as the structure and practices of negotiation also had a bearing. If these latter factors did, as some of the panelists believed, then removing structural impediments could make multilateral negotiations more likely to achieve effective outcomes with limited political attention and resource.

EXPANDING THE SCOPE OF PARTICIPATION

It was noted that, compared with many other fields of multilateral activity, some disarmament arms control processes lacked civil society involvement. At the same time, transnational civil society involvement raised a host of issues, one panelist noted. Although civil society engagement in processes such as the 1997 Antipersonnel Mine Ban Convention had been extensive and positive, there were other cases (such as tobacco control treaty negotiations) when NGOs had at times risked calling their independence or credibility into question and this might even have been to the detriment of the consensus building process. Several participants agreed that it was quite difficult to generalize about NGO characteristics: the small arms process, for instance, had revealed a wide range of NGO views on private firearm possession by civilians, for instance. More analysis needed to be done to understand the NGO impacts on negotiations, which could vary in specific instances.

It was also noted that while transnational civil society represented a form of world public conscience it was still predominantly a Western phenomenon. In some countries truly independent civil society voices had yet to be manifested. Their absence in some domestic political cultures had resulted in resistance to civil society participation in arms control and disarmament negotiations. Discussions also underscored the need for international cooperation and benchmark setting within the NGO community to allow for their more effective engagement with states and to optimize the chances of their concerns and opinions being voiced effectively at the decision-making level.

During the course of discussions participants raised the issue of the engagement of the humanitarian community in arms control and disarmament processes. There was recognition that there was currently a persistent degree of disconnection between these two communities resulting in limited awareness of the other's work. If practitioners in these fields were to interact with each other in a meaningful way there needed to be more information-sharing, it was suggested.

ANALYSING THE ROLES OF EXISTING PARTICIPANTS IN MULTILATERAL NEGOTIATION PROCESSES

Attention was paid to difficulties in analysing the roles of multilateral negotiating practitioners from outside the processes in which they operated. This was not solely a question of insufficient transparency (although this too was an issue in processes such as the Conference on Disarmament). However transparent a negotiating process was to those outside, it could be expected that endgame negotiating would be done privately between governmental representatives. Individual negotiators were usually neither plenipotentiary nor passive mouthpieces of the states they represented, but on a spectrum in various places in between. Individual negotiators, it was observed, often could and do a lot to influence the policies and positions of their respective governments and sometimes those of others. This was something that needed to be explored further, it was thought.

OTHER POINTS

There appeared to be a general feeling that new and innovative approaches were needed to address current problems in arms control and disarmament. It was observed that while many governments had stated the need to "think outside the box" in terms of making multilateral processes in this domain more effective, this had not necessarily translated into many specific improvements and it was noted that the disarmament as humanitarian project could have a role to play there.

It was also observed that there remained lack of agreement over what features of multilateral disarmament and arms control constituted problems and what action should be taken. Rules of procedure, for instance, were often problems for some actors in negotiations but not for others able to deploy them to their own advantage.

By the conclusion of discussions, the important function that multilateral disarmament and arms control institutions and negotiating processes played in the creation of international norms had been underscored.

RECENT UNIDIR PUBLICATIONS[1]

Multilateral Diplomacy and the NPT: An Insider's Account, by Jayantha Dhanapala with Randy Rydell, in cooperation with SIPRI, 2005, 206p., United Nations publication, Sales No. GV.E.05.0.5.

Peace in the Middle East: P2P and the Israeli-Palestinian Conflict, by Adel Atieh, Gilad Ben-Nun, Gasser El Shahed, Rana Taha and Steve Tulliu, 2004, 54p., United Nations publication, Sales No. GV.E.05.0.2.

Building a Weapons of Mass Destruction Free Zone in the Middle East: Global Non-Proliferation Regimes and Regional Experiences, in cooperation with the League of Arab States, 2004, 310p., United Nations publication, Sales No. GV.E.04.0.30.

Implementing the United Nations Programme of Action on Small Arms and Light Weapons: Analysis of the Reports Submitted by States in 2003, by Elli Kytömäki and Valerie Anne Yankey-Wayne, in cooperation with UNDP, DDA and SAS, 2004, 320p., United Nations publication, Sales No. GV.E.04.0.27.

Open Skies: A Cooperative Approach to Military Transparency and Confidence Building, by Pál Dunay, Márton Krasznai, Hartwig Spitzer, Rafael Wiemker and William Wynne, 2004, 340p., United Nations publication, Sales No. GV.E.04.0.18.

A Guide to the Destruction of Small Arms and Light Weapons—The Approach of the South African National Defence Force, by Sarah Meek and Noel Stott, in cooperation with SAS, 2004, 76p., United Nations publication, Sales No. GV.E.04.0.5.

Costs of Disarmament—Mortgaging the Future: The South Asian Arms Dynamic, by Susan Willett, 2004, 124p., United Nations publication, Sales No. GV.E.04.0.1.

---

[1] For a complete list, please see our Web site at http://www.unidir.org, or contact Anita Blétry: Tel.: +41(0)22 917 42 63, Fax: +41 (0)22 917 01 76, abletry@unog.ch.

After Non-Detection, What?—What Iraq's Unfound WMD Mean for the Future of Non-Proliferation, by Michael Friend, 2003, 32p., United Nations publication, UNIDIR/2003/38.

Outer Space and Global Security, in cooperation with Ploughshares and Simons Centre for Peace and Disarmament Studies, 2003, 104p., United Nations publication, Sales No. GV.E.03.0.26.

Costs of Disarmament—Disarming the Costs: Nuclear Arms Control and Nuclear Rearmament, by Susan Willett, 2003, 174p., United Nations publication, Sales No. GV.E.03.0.25.

Desarme nuclear: Regímenes internacional, latinoaméricano y argentino de no proliferación, por Marcelo F. Valle Fonrouge, 2003, 146p., United Nations publication, Sales No. GV.S.03.0.24.

Coming to Terms with Security: A Lexicon for Arms Control, Disarmament and Confidence-Building, by Steve Tulliu and Thomas Schmalberger, 2003, 252p., United Nations publication, Sales No. GV.E/A.03.0.21.

* Also available in Arabic, 278p., Sales No. GV.E/A.03.0.21.
* Also available in Spanish, 548p., Sales No. GV.E/S.03.0.29.
* Also available in Korean, 626p., UNIDIR/2003/30.

Destroying Surplus Weapons: An Assessment of Experience in South Africa and Lesotho, by Sarah Meek and Noel Stott, in coooperation with SAS, 2003, 102p., United Nations publication, Sales No. GV.E.03.0.18.

Lutte contre la prolifération des armes légPres en Afrique de l'Ouest: Manuel de formation des forces armées et de sécurité, sous la direction de Anatole Ayissi et Ibrahima Sall, en coopération avec le PCASED et la CEDEAO, 2003, 150p., publication des Nations Unies, numéro de vente: GV.F.03.0.17.

Coming to Terms with Security: A Handbook on Verification and Compliance, in cooperation with VERTIC, 2003, 158p., United Nations publication, Sales No. GV.E/A.03.0.12.

* Also available in Arabic, 172p., Sales No. GV.E/A.03.0.12.

Internal Conflict and Regional Security in South Asia: Approaches, Perspectives and Policies, by Shiva Hari Dahal, Haris Gazdar, S.I. Keethaponcalan and Padmaja Murthy, 2003, 62p., United Nations publication, Sales No. GV.E.03.0.10.

The Scope and Implications of a Tracing Mechanism for Small Arms and Light Weapons, in cooperation with SAS, 2003, 238p., United Nations publication, Sales No. GV.E.03.0.7.

* Existe également en français: ***Portée et implications d'un mécanisme de traçage des armes légères et de petit calibre***, en coopération avec SAS, 2003, 264p., publication des Nations Unies, numéro de vente: GV.F.03.0.07.

Participatory Monitoring of Humanitarian Mine Action: Giving Voice to Citizens of Nicaragua, Mozambique and Cambodia, by Susan Willett (ed.), 2003, 122p., United Nations publication, Sales No. GV.E.03.0.6.

The Treaty of Pelindaba on the African Nuclear-Weapon-Free Zone, by Oluyemi Adeniji, 2002, 332p., United Nations publication, Sales No. GV.E.03.0.5.

Project Coast: Apartheid's Chemical and Biological Warfare Programme, by Chandré Gould and Peter Folb, in cooperation with the Centre for Conflict Resolution, 2002, 300p., United Nations publication, Sales No. GV.E.02.0.10.

Tactical Nuclear Weapons: Time for Control, by Taina Susiluoto, 2002, 162p., United Nations publication, Sales No. GV.E.02.0.7.

Le Conseil de sécurité à l'aube du XXIème siècle : quelle volonté et quelle capacité a-t-il de maintenir la paix et la sécurité internationales ?, par Pascal Teixeira, en coopération avec l'IFRI, 2002, 106p., publication des Nations Unies, numéro de vente: GV.F.02.0.6.

* Also available in English: ***The Security Council at the Dawn of the Twenty-First Century: To What Extent Is It Willing and Able to Maintain International Peace and Security?***, by Pascal Teixeira, in cooperation with IFRI, 2003, 135p., United Nations publication, Sales No. GV.E.02.0.6.

Costs of Disarmament—Rethinking the Price Tag: A Methodological Inquiry into the Cost and Benefits of Arms Control, by Susan Willett, 2002, 70p., United Nations publication, Sales No. GV.E.02.0.3.

Missile Defence, Deterrence and Arms Control: Contradictory Aims or Compatible Goals?, in cooperation with Wilton Park, 2002, 39p., United Nations publication, UNIDIR/2002/4.

Disarmament as Humanitarian Action—A discussion on the occasion of the 20th anniversary of the United Nations Institute for Disarmament Research (UNIDIR), in cooperation with the United Nations Department for Disarmament Affairs (DDA), 2001, 24p., United Nations publication, UNIDIR/2001/23.

* Existe également en français: *Le désarmement comme action humanitaire*, en coopération avec le Département des affaires de

désarmement de l'Organisation des Nations Unies, 2003, 30p., United Nations publication, UNIDIR/2003/7.

Cooperating for Peace in West Africa: An Agenda for the 21st Century, by Anatole Ayissi (ed.), 2001, 159p., United Nations publication, Sales No. GV.E/F.01.0.19 / *Coopération pour la paix en Afrique de l'Ouest : Agenda pour le XXIème siècle*, sous la direction d'Anatole Ayissi, 2001, 169p., publication des Nations Unies, numéro de vente : GV.E/F.01.0.19.

Illicit Trafficking in Firearms: Prevention and Combat in Rio de Janeiro, Brazil—A National, Regional and Global Issue, by Péricles Gasparini Alves, 2000, 66p., United Nations publication, Sales No. GV.E.01.0.2.

Tactical Nuclear Weapons: A Perspective from Ukraine, by A. Shevtsov, A. Yizhak, A. Gavrish and A. Chumakov, 2001, 95p., United Nations publication, Sales No. GV.E.01.0.1.

Tactical Nuclear Weapons: Options for Control, by William C. Potter, Nikolai Sokov, Harald Müller and Annette Schaper, 2000, 87p., United Nations publication, Sales No. GV.E.00.0.21.

Bound to Cooperate: Conflict, Peace and People in Sierra Leone, by Anatole Ayissi and Robin-Edward Poulton (eds), 2000, 213p., United Nations publication, Sales No. GV.E.00.0.20.

Coming to Terms with Security: A Lexicon for Arms Control, Disarmament and Confidence-Building, by Steve Tulliu and Thomas Schmalberger, 2000, 246p., United Nations publication, Sales No. GV.E.00.0.12.

The Small Arms Problem in Central Asia: Features and Implications, by Bobi Pirseyedi, 2000, 120p., United Nations publication, Sales No. GV.E.00.0.6.

Peacekeeping in Africa: Capabilities and Culpabilities, by Eric G. Berman and Katie E. Sams, 2000, 540p., United Nations publication, Sales No. GV.E.00.0.4.

West Africa Small Arms Moratorium: High-Level Consultations on the Modalities for the Implementation of PCASED, by Jacqueline Seck, 2000, 81p., United Nations publication, UNIDIR/2000/2 / *Moratoire ouest-africain sur les armes légères : Consultations de haut niveau sur les modalités de la mise en œuvre du PCASED*, par Jacqueline Seck, 2000, 83p., United Nations publication, UNIDIR/2000/2.

Disarmament Forum / *Forum du désarmement*
(quarterly / trimestriel)